Marjorie Briggs IV

THE TEACH YOURSELF BOOKS

BIOLOGY

TEACH YOURSELF

BIOLOGY

M. E. PHILLIPS, B.Sc.

L. E. COX, B.Sc., F.L.S.

THE ENGLISH UNIVERSITIES PRESS LTD
ST PAUL'S HOUSE WARWICK LANE
LONDON EC4

First printed 1940
New edition 1951
This impression 1968

S.B.N. 340 05525 1

Printed and bound for the English Universities Press Ltd., by Richard Clay (The Chaucer Press), Ltd., Bungay, Suffolk

PREFACE

To the student of Biology is given the chance of gaining a wider knowledge of " self " and therefore of obeying, to a limited degree, that most difficult dictum " Know Thyself ".

Such knowledge must necessarily be incomplete, but it becomes somewhat fuller when instead of centring round one organism only, the " self ", it includes at least a passing acquaintanceship with the wide world of living things.

Aristotle (384–322 B.C.) writes " . . . one should not be childishly contemptuous of the most insignificant animals. For every realm of nature is marvellous ". Neither must the " most insignificant " plants be neglected in undertaking a survey of the whole business of living.

Much fuller meaning is given to biological study when thoughtful reading is accompanied by practical work. For this reason instructions are given in the text for the carrying out of simple experiments with the minimum of apparatus. The apparatus suggested includes a drawing board and drawing pins, scissors, a scalpel or other sharp knife, a small bottle of formalin, glass slides and cover slips, a thistle funnel, pig's bladder, a gas jar, and a hand lens; if a microscope is available, it will be a useful addition, but all the practical work indicated in the book can be carried out without its help.

M. E. P.
L. E. C.

London.

CONTENTS

CONTENTS

SECTION III

THE WIDE WORLD OF LIVING THINGS : THEIR STRUCTURE, RANGE, AND VARIETY

SECTION IV

EVOLUTION AND HEREDITY

LIST OF FIGURES

SECTION I

THE ANIMAL AS A MACHINE INCESSANTLY AT WORK

CHAPTER I

FEEDING : THE DIGESTIVE SYSTEM

MANY busy people will be content to " teach themselves biology " by merely reading what is written in a book. Others who have more time, or a more inquiring mind, will like to see things for themselves, and for their guidance suggestions are made in the following pages for carrying out simple experiments, and instructions are given for dissections that can easily be done at home.

To most of us our " self " is of great importance, and it is this " self " that has been chosen as the approach to the subject.

A gathering of unscientific people, of at least average intelligence, was recently discussing various topics of general interest. In the course of conversation the question was asked : " What is the use of blood in the body ? " After a pause one member answered : " Well, it just goes round and round."

Although this statement is undoubtedly true, it does not lead one very far. The circulation of blood is not " just " a purposeless meandering.

Every minutest living part of the body must be fed, and every minutest part of living tissue must breathe. Therefore food and oxygen must be carried to all parts. With the exception of very lowly organisms animals have a blood-stream, and it is this that acts as the transport system, carrying oxygen and food.

Three basic necessities of the life of an individual are therefore obvious :—

1. Food that is eaten must, in some way, be brought into such a state that it can be carried by the blood to all parts of the body, making growth possible and repairing waste. This is the work of *digestion*.

2. Oxygen that is inhaled must be absorbed by the blood, which must then carry it to, and give it up to, the tissues. This is part of the work of *respiration*.

3. The blood must pass through all tissues, and therefore be in constant movement. This is the work of *circulation*, which is controlled by the heart.

In the first two sections of this book the workings of the bodily " machine " of the higher plants and animals are described and explained. Divergences in simple organisms are deferred until Section III.

The actual digestive system cannot be studied by the ordinary layman in a human being. Man is one member of a large class of animals known as *Mammals*. One distinguishing characteristic of the class is that there are mammary glands in the female, by means of which the young are fed with milk. One all-too-common mammal is the rat, and, for the sake of cheapness, it is often used in dissection. It is, however, an unpleasant animal to deal with, and a little obnoxious to most of us. A rabbit is more expensive, but is much pleasanter to operate upon. A rabbit bought from the poulterer is not a good " subject ", for, whether it has been trapped or shot, certain vital parts will certainly have been injured. The best course is to buy, from a recognized dealer in biological material, a rabbit that has been chloroformed. If it is kept in a $2\frac{1}{2}$ per cent. solution of formalin in water, it can be used again and

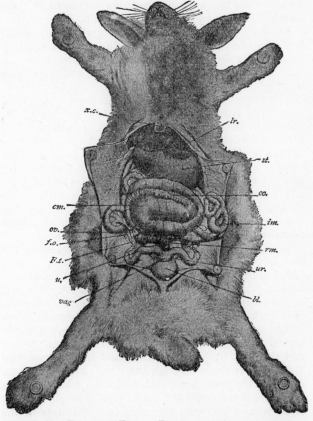

Fig. 1.—The Body of a Female Rabbit with Abdomen Opened, the Organs being Displaced as Little as Possible.

bl., bladder; *cm.*, cæcum; *co.*, colon; *F.t.*, Fallopian tube; *f.o.*, fimbriated opening of the oviduct; *im.*, ileum; *lr.*, liver; *ov.*, ovary; *rm.*, rectum; *st.*, stomach; *ur.*, ureter; *u.*, right uterus; *vag.*, vagina; *x.c.*, xiphoid cartilage. " *Manual of Elementary Zoology*", by *L. A. Borradaile* (*Oxford University Press*).

again for all the work of dissection suggested in these pages. (See p. 52 for treatment of brain.)

The only part of the rabbit that is at all unpleasant is the digestive tract. Partly for this reason, and partly because it is the region first exposed on dissection, it is well to begin a practical study with this, and then throw it away.

The Digestive Tract.—The rabbit should be pinned to a board lying on its back, that is on its *dorsal* side; the *ventral* part of the animal is then uppermost. The fur of the ventral surface must be cut up the middle as far as the chest, and separated from the body with the handle of a scalpel. Two lateral cuts are then made at the forward end, giving flaps that can be turned back and pinned to the board for greater security. The pinkish flesh that is exposed when the fur is removed is the body-wall, and if it is similarly cut and pinned back, the rabbit looks like the picture in Fig. 1.

Deep-red lobes of the liver are seen overlying the stomach, which is bulky with undigested food. There are about 8 feet of digestive tract compactly coiled, and held in place by a thin, glistening tissue. All this part of the body in which the intestine lies is the *abdomen*. It is limited towards the head end of the animal by an arched muscular partition; this is the *diaphragm*, which should not yet be injured. Between the diaphragm and the neck the fur can be cut and turned back, and a careful cut made through the ribs. In this way the cavity of the chest is exposed, and a flat whitish tube is seen to extend down the neck, pass through the diaphragm, and lead into the stomach. This tube is the gullet, or *œsophagus*, through which food passes to the stomach from the mouth.

With care and a little skill it is now possible to remove the whole digestive tract and lay it out on a board as shown in Fig. 2. The glistening tissue must first be carefully torn away with the handle of the scalpel. The various coils will then tend to spread apart. Between diaphragm and stomach the gullet should be cut across. A second cut across the gut at the far end of the body leaves the tract free in the abdomen. In disentangling the coils and arranging the length on the board, careful handling is necessary if breaks are to be avoided.

In the process of digestion partly digested food passes

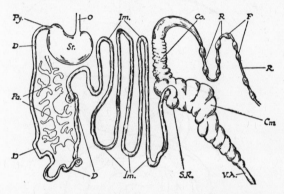

FIG. 2.—THE ALIMENTARY TRACT OF THE RABBIT REMOVED AND ARRANGED TO SHOW ALL THE PARTS CLEARLY.

Cm., *Co.*, *R.*, parts of the large intestine; *F.*, fæces; *D.*, duodenum; *Im.*, *S.R.*, parts of the small intestine; *O.*, œsophagus; *Pa.*, pancreas; *Py.*, pylorus; *St.*, stomach; *V.A.*, vermiform appendix.

from the stomach into the small intestine. This is a very long bit of tract, and is only called "small" because of its narrow diameter. The first part forms a U-shaped loop enclosing a soft, pinkish mass of glandular tissue, the *pancreas*; it is this tissue of sheep and oxen that is sold as "sweetbread". The small intestine enters the large intestine at right angles, in such a way that one part of the large intestine ends blindly (Fig. 2), terminating in the *vermiform appendix* that may cause so much trouble in the human body, where it is very small (Fig. 3). The trouble is caused by bits of hard

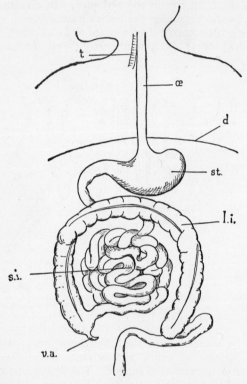

FIG. 3.—DIAGRAM OF ALIMENTARY CANAL OF MAN.
d., diaphragm; *l.i.*, large intestine; *œ.*, œsophagus; *s.i.*, small intestine; *st.*, stomach; *t.*, trachea; *v.a.*, vermiform appendix.

food finding their way through the narrow opening of the appendix, and setting up inflammation. The main part of the large intestine ends at the *anus*, an opening through which the waste products of digestion are expelled.

In the fully grown human body the digestive, or *alimentary*, tract is about 20 feet in length, but a comparison of the drawing in Fig. 3 with that of the dissection of the rabbit, or with Fig. 2, shows that the parts are essentially the same. As well as being the same in appearance, the different parts of the tract carry on similar work in rabbit and in man.

To realize just what this work is, the course of a light meal can be followed, from the entry of the food into the mouth, to the expulsion of undigested waste matter at the anus.

Foodstuffs are of three classes, which differ from one another in chemical composition :—

    1. *Carbohydrates*, which are mainly energy-giving foods, and include sugars, starch and cellulose.

    2. *Proteins*, which are mainly body-builders. They include lean meat, white of egg, the glutinous part of all cereal foods, and the bulk of cheese.

    3. *Fats*, which provide the body with heat. Fat meat, butter, and all oils are included in this class of foodstuffs.

The light meal that is suggested must have something of all these foods : a " snack " of a glass of milk and a sandwich of ham and water-cress contains proteins in the lean ham, the bread, and the milk; fats (the butter, the fat of the ham, and the fats of the milk); carbohydrates (the starch of the bread, the sugars of the milk, the cellulose of the cress); water (chiefly in the cress and the milk); inorganic salts (in the cress); and, finally, vitamins (p. 24) in milk, butter, and cress.

Digestion begins in the mouth when the teeth crush

and grind the food and saliva flows upon it. The action of the saliva is to change the starch of the food into sugar. This can be tasted if a piece of dry bread is thoroughly chewed for some time before it is swallowed. A little piece of laundry starch allowed to rest on the back of the tongue also begins to taste sweet because of the action of saliva.

When the chewed mass is swallowed it leaves the mouth for the gullet, which loses its flat appearance and becomes tubular. By way of the gullet the food reaches the stomach. It is obvious that no substance can pass along some 9 or 10 inches of tubing unless pressure is in some way brought to bear upon it. In the wall of the gullet, and of all the rest of the intestine, there are certain *longitudinal muscles* disposed along the length of the tract, and others, *circular muscles*, that have a hooplike arrangement around the tube. The muscles are stimulated to *peristaltic* action by the pressure of the bulky food on the gullet-wall, and by their alternate contraction and expansion the food is pushed along. Pinching a pea along a length of rubber tubing gives a rough representation of the movement.

By the time the suggested " snack " reaches the stomach its character is somewhat altered : the milk is unchanged, but the bread is partly digested, the fats are partially melted, the lean ham and the water-cress are ground up.

In the wall of the stomach, in addition to the longitudinal and circular muscles, there is a third set arranged diagonally. These give rise to a gentle rocking, churnlike motion, as a result of which every particle of food in the stomach is covered with digestive juices produced by glands in its wall.

The special substances that bring about digestion are known as *ferments*, or *enzymes*. It was the action of a special enzyme in the saliva that caused some of the starch in the bread to turn to sugar. Within a living animal or plant chemical changes are always taking place which, outside, can occur only at temperatures so high as to make life impossible. Certain substances, termed *catalysts*, have the power of increasing the rate at which chemical changes take place, but catalysts cannot actually induce these changes. The action of enzymes is catalytic. The conversion of starch $(C_6H_{10}O_5)$ into sugar $(C_6H_{12}O_6)$ is produced by the combination of a water molecule (H_2O) with a molecule of starch. This process is termed *hydrolysis*, and the largest and best-known group of enzymes bring about hydrolytic action.

As yet no pure enzyme has been isolated, and their chemical constitution is unknown. It is probable that they are protein in nature; they generally contain the elements carbon, hydrogen, oxygen and nitrogen. They are always produced in the living cell, but nothing is known as to their mode of origin. They can be extracted from the living cell and kept for an indefinite period without losing their catalytic power. In many cases their action is specific, a particular enzyme bringing about only one chemical reaction. Several enzymes may be present in the same cell; a large number have been extracted from yeast (p. 132).

The glands of the stomach secrete two enzymes—*pepsin*, which begins the digestion of proteins; and *rennin*, which curdles milk.

Pepsin is a familiar term nowadays, because sufferers from digestive ailments are frequently ordered " peptonized " food—that is food that has already been acted upon by pepsin, extracted from the glands of sheep or oxen. When such peptonized food is eaten, the stomach is relieved of some of its work.

" Rennin " is not an altogether unfamiliar term, because " rennet " is used in making junket. The milk, slightly warmed, is treated with a preparation of rennin in tablet or liquid form, and junket results. This is an entirely similar action to that which takes place in the stomach, where, also, the milk is at a higher temperature than that of the atmosphere.

Solidification of milk in the stomach is necessary because it is much more than a mere liquid, and it must be retained until the pepsin has digested the protein it contains.

The glands of the stomach also produce hydrochloric acid, which is essential because the action of pepsin can only take place in an acid medium. Also the acid helps to keep the stomach comparatively free from germs. It is the greater proportion of acid in their digestive juices that explains the power of dogs to digest bone.

Periodically a muscular ring that closes the passage between stomach and small intestine relaxes, and through the opening such food as is ready for further digestion enters the first intestinal loop.

Here digestive juices containing three different enzymes are poured upon it from the pancreas and, by way of the bile-duct, bile reaches it from the liver. One pancreatic enzyme completes the change of starch into sugar; another acts on the partly digested proteins; the third emulsifies the fats and decomposes them with the formation of fatty acids and glycerine. Bile co-operates with the pancreatic juice in digesting and emulsifying fats. In the further passage along the intestine the proteins are acted upon by yet another enzyme, which makes them completely soluble.

The semi-liquid stream in the small intestine bears no resemblance to the original " snack ". Starch has been changed into sugar. Fatty acids, glycerine, and soluble soaps have taken the place of the fats of the ham, milk, and butter. The proteins of the lean ham and of the bread and milk have been changed to simpler soluble substances. Only the cellulose of the cress remains unchanged; this, like all green vegetable food, has played its part as " roughage " in stimulating the muscles. In rabbits and other vegetable-feeders cellulose is digested by certain enzymes that are not produced in the alimentary tract of man.

Sickness results when change in nervous control makes muscular action work in an opposite direction from the normal, with the result that food travels backward. In sheep and cattle this *antiperistalsis* is a normal procedure. After a period of cropping and swallowing the grass, muscular action is reversed, the crushed and partly digested food is returned to the mouth, and the animals then chew the cud.

That part of the liquid stream which will prove serviceable in promoting growth and repairing waste is carried out of the intestine and is distributed to all parts of the body. The lining of the intestine is plush-like, because countless numbers of delicate, finger-like processes, called *villi*, extend from the wall. Each villus contains a colourless *lacteal tube* whose work is noted below, and also *blood capillaries* which are the finest imaginable branches of arteries and veins. Digested proteins and carbohydrates enter the blood by diffusing into the villi and into their capillaries, along which they are conducted outwards through the intestinal wall. This digested food then passes into larger and larger vessels, until it finally reaches the large *portal*, or carrying vein.

Before the alimentary tract is removed from the rabbit, veins can be seen in the glistening connective tissue, radiating out in fan-like fashion from the intestine to the portal vein, by which proteins and carbohydrates are carried to the liver to be stored until they are needed.

Fats enter the blood-stream in a much more roundabout way. They pass into the lacteal tubes of the villi, which unite outside the alimentary canal to form a large *lacteal vessel*. This runs forward in the body, and opens into the left jugular vein in the neck; in this somewhat indirect way fats are carried to the blood for distribution to the tissues.

The residue left in the intestine when carbohydrates, proteins, and fats have been removed passes into the large intestine. It is in a very liquid state, because so many digestive juices have been poured upon it in the journey from the mouth. In the large intestine much of the watery medium is absorbed by the blood, so that the waste matter becomes more solid. As *fæces* it passes along the intestine to the terminal opening, the anus; this is closed by a ring of muscles, which relax when the waste is expelled. In Fig. 2 the pellet-like fæces of the rabbit are seen at the end of the intestine.

In recent years experimental work has proved that growth may be neither normal nor healthy, even when food has been taken in the right proportions and in the right amount. Something more than food is necessary.

The additional, indispensable factors are *vitamins*, which occur in exceedingly small quantities in certain articles of food. According to differences in their properties and chemical composition, they are classed as A, B, C, D, E, etc.

Of these A, D, and E are soluble in fat, and occur, for instance, in butter, and in most animal fats. A is also present in eggs, the embryos of seeds, and green vegetables. It is essential for the healthy growth of young animals in particular, and plays an important part in creating immunity to various diseases.

Although A is soluble in fats it is not present in lard; its absence is explained by the fact that pigs do not eat grass. When A is absent from the diet of an individual he readily " catches " diseases due to bacteria; he is prone to colds and influenza; eye-trouble, too, results from the absence of A in food.

If they are not provided with vitamin D young animals suffer from rickets, and have bad teeth. Children brought up in over-crowded districts, where sunlight is lacking, often suffer from rickets, and their bones and teeth do not develop normally. A diet rich in D counteracts this " deficiency disease ", which is also prevented by ultra-violet radiation, because these rays lead to the presence of D in the skin. This explains the value of sun-bathing. Pigs are very liable to be rickety; it is for this reason that, in Norway and Sweden, many pig-breeders have windows in the stys fitted with glass that transmits ultra-violet light.

Vitamin E is present in wheat, milk, lettuces and green leaves generally. Its absence affects the reproductive organs and leads to sterility: no young rats were born of female rats that had been brought up on a diet deficient in E.

Vitamins B and C are soluble in water, and are widely distributed in fresh fruit and vegetables. Constipation and various nervous diseases arise in the absence of B, of which two forms are distinguished, classed as B_1 and B_2. The lack of B_1 is responsible for " beri-beri ", a disease that is common among Japanese peasants, who live largely on polished rice. This lacks B_1, which occurs in the outer layers only of rice grains and other cereals; these layers are absent in the polished rice.

Scurvy is prevented by vitamin C. This vitamin disappears completely in all canned and preserved foods, a fact that explains why, in the past, scurvy was such a scourge among passengers on long voyages. Bottle-fed babies sometimes develop scurvy because the vitamins their milk contains have been destroyed by over-boiling. If they are given orange- or grape-juice regularly the deficiency of vitamins in the milk is counteracted.

CHAPTER II

CIRCULATION: THE HEART AND THE NATURE OF BLOOD

NOWADAYS " blood transfusion " is a familiar term, and most hospitals have a list of men and women who will come forward, when summoned, to allow blood to be passed from their blood-vessels into those of a patient in urgent need.

In the *plasma*, or liquid part of the blood, there are two kinds of minute bodies, or *corpuscles*—these are the red corpuscles and the white. In a drop of blood smeared on a glass slide, and looked at under the microscope, many minute yellowish bodies are seen. These are the " red " corpuscles which, in the mass, give blood its characteristic colour. The white corpuscles are not easy to distinguish, partly because of their lack of colour, but still more because they are so greatly outnumbered by the red; the proportion of red corpuscles to white is approximately 500 to 1.

The white corpuscles differ both in size and function. Some may escape from the blood-stream and travel to an area where *bacteria*, or " germs ", are causing a scratch or a wound to fester; here the white corpuscles engulf the bacteria; the matter, or *pus*, that accumulates at the spot contains the corpuscles and the germs they have absorbed. Smaller white corpuscles in the blood set up a chemical defence against infectious diseases. Others, again, bring about clotting, and so prevent excessive loss of blood after an injury.

Unlike the white corpuscles, the red are uniform in size and function. Their work is to absorb oxygen that reaches the lungs from the outside air and carry it to all parts of the body. The oxygen is absorbed by the *hæmoglobin* of the corpuscles, forming *oxyhæmoglobin* which is brilliantly red.

These general statements are true of the blood of all human beings. There are, however, beyond this general uniformity, certain differences on which the classification of blood into four groups depends. In blood-transfusion it is essential that the blood of the donor should be of the same group as that of the recipient.

There are some people—the " universal donors "— whose blood shows no antagonism to the other three. In successful operations the value of transfusion is two-fold : in the first place, a patient who has lost blood has the volume of the plasma restored, and receives the salts and proteins that are associated with it ; in the second place, fresh red corpuscles are introduced to make up the patient's deficiency.

" Stored blood " is widely used in transfusion operations. It is withdrawn in a sterile condition and infection is prevented from reaching it. After about two weeks the red corpuscles of stored blood break down and produce substances that would be poisonous to a re-cipient. It has been found possible to remove the red corpuscles from blood withdrawn from a donor, and to dry the resultant plasma so that it can be kept in a stored condition for a very long time. The dried plasma can be mixed with distilled sterilised water and used for transfusion in cases of emergency.

In the human body red corpuscles are formed by division of cells (p. 113) in the red marrow of bones. It is estimated that the length of life of an individual corpuscle is about three weeks. The destruction of the corpuscles takes place largely in the spleen. A certain number are also destroyed in the liver. It is the dead corpuscles that give the characteristic colour to bile and that account for the yellowish colour of the fæces.

The plasma of the blood of one individual, A, may be antagonistic to the red corpuscles of another individual,

B, destroying the hæmoglobin of B's red corpuscles, with the result that they can no longer carry oxygen. If this were to happen in the body of a patient he would die, because he would be deprived of oxygen. Therefore the quality of the blood of all volunteers for transfusion must be listed by the hospitals.

In order to carry out its various functions the blood

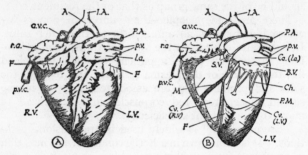

FIG. 4.—A, SHEEP'S HEART (DIAGRAMMATIC). B, THE SAME: PART OF THE WALLS OF THE VENTRICLES AND THE LEFT AURICLE CUT AWAY.

a.v.c., anterior vena cava; *A.*, aortic arch; *B.V.*, bicuspid valve; *Ca.*, cavity of auricle; *Ch.*, chordæ tendineæ; *Cv.*, cavity of ventricle; *F.*, fat; *I.A.*, innominate artery; *l.a.*, left auricle; *L.V.*, left ventricle; *M.*, moderator band; *P.A.*, pulmonary artery; *P.M.*, muscles at base of tendonous cords; *p.v.*, pulmonary vein; *p.v.c.*, posterior vena cava; *r.a.*, right auricle; *R.V.*, right ventricle; *S.V.*, semi-lunar valves of pulmonary artery.

must be in constant movement. This movement depends upon the action of the heart.

To understand how the heart works it is advisable to get from the butcher one of a good size, such as that of a sheep. The detailed structure of such a heart is seen in Fig. 4.

On the ventral surface there is a groove filled with fat which marks the division between the two largest chambers of the four-chambered heart; these are the right and left *ventricles*. The tip of the latter forms the apex of the heart.

The blood-vessels of the body are either *arteries* or *veins*. Arteries carry blood *away* from the heart, while veins carry blood *to* the heart.

Blood is driven from the heart by the contraction of the strong muscular walls of the ventricles, and is forced into arteries which are in open communication with each ventricle at the end away from its apex. Through the *aorta* oxygenated blood, expelled from the *left* ventricle, enters an arterial system that carries it to all parts of the body. From the *right* ventricle the *pulmonary* artery carries blood, that has lost much of its oxygen, to the lungs, where the hæmoglobin of its red corpuscles takes up a fresh oxygen supply.

If a pencil is passed through the cut ends of the aortic and pulmonary arteries, it will pass into the ventricle with which each communicates. If the little finger is pushed into the cut end of either artery, it will be tightly gripped by the muscular arterial wall.

The other two chambers of the heart are the right and left *auricles*. They are flabby and puckered, and the veins which enter them are readily distinguishable from the arteries which leave the ventricles, because the walls of veins are not nearly so muscular.

It is by way of the veins that blood which has given up oxygen to, and received carbon dioxide from, all parts of the body is returned to the heart, entering it through the *right* auricle. Veins from the head, face, neck, and arms unite on one side to form the *left precaval* vein, and on the other side the *right precaval* vein is similarly formed (Fig. 5). (In the sheep the two precavals unite before their entry into the auricle.) The *postcaval* vein brings blood to the auricle from the hind part of the body.

The blood which enters the *left* auricle comes directly from the lungs, and is therefore highly oxygenated.

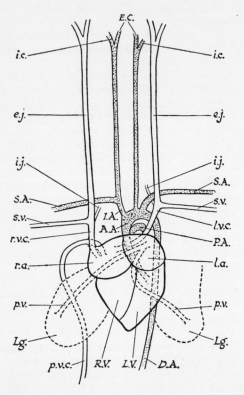

Fig. 5.—Diagram of Arteries (Shaded) and Veins in the Anterior Part of the Body of a Mammal (Rabbit).

A.A., aortic arch; *D.A.*, dorsal aorta; *E.C.*, external carotid; *e.j.*, external jugular; *I.A.*, innominate; *i.c.*, internal carotid; *i.j.*, internal jugular; *l.a.*, left auricle; *Lg.*, lung; *L.V.*, left ventricle; *l.v.c.*, left anterior vena cava; *P.A.*, pulmonary artery; *p.v.*, pulmonary vein; *p.v.c.*, posterior vena cava; *r.a.*, right auricle; *R.V.*, right ventricle; *r.v.c.*, right anterior vena cava; *S.A.*, subclavian artery; *s.v.*, subclavian vein.

The flow of blood from the right auricle to the right ventricle, and from the left auricle to the left ventricle, is controlled by flap-like valves, which now shut off auricle from ventricle, and now leave open communication between them.

To understand how this happens, part of the right auricle should be cut away, just leaving its base as a cup-like rim. Water from a tap may be run into this, to imitate the flow of blood from the caval veins. As the water passes from the auricle and fills the ventricle, three flaps, which were hanging down in the cavity of the ventricle, are seen to rise and close the communication between auricle and ventricle, forming, as it were, a floor to the one and a roof to the other. In life this valvular action prevents a back-flow from ventricles to auricles when the muscular walls of the ventricles contract, and thus exert pressure upon the blood within them. The flow from auricle to ventricle, on the right and left of the heart, is simultaneous, and the sounds of the heart's beat are probably partly due to the click of the closing valves.

Where they are connected with auricles and ventricles the veins and arteries are fairly wide tubes, but their final branches, in the various tissues of the body, may have a diameter of only one-three-thousandth $(\frac{1}{3000})$ part of an inch.

These ultimate branches are the *capillaries*, which have very thin, delicate walls. Sometimes as the result of a knock—on the flesh of arm or leg, for instance— some of the capillary walls are broken, and blood escapes into the tissues forming a " bruise ", whose changing colours are due to the fact that the escaped blood is giving up oxygen and is therefore losing its red colour (p. 27), and is passing through various shades until the bruise is " black and blue ".

It only requires a little skill, but much patience, to dissect the rabbit preserved in formalin, so that its veins and arteries may be seen as clearly as in Figs. 5, 6, and 7. The animal must be pinned down on its back, and cuts must be made through the ribs to expose the heart, which lies in the cavity of the chest, or *thorax*, enclosed

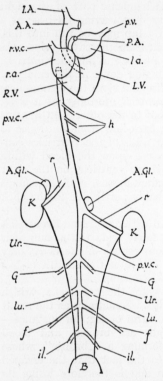

FIG. 6.—THE CHIEF POSTERIOR VEINS OF A MAMMAL (RABBIT).

A.A., aortic arch; *A.Gl.*, adrenal gland; *B.*, bladder; *f.*, femoral; *g.*, genital; *h.*, hepatic; *I.A.*, innominate artery; *il.*, internal iliac; *K.*, kidney; *lu.*, ilio-lumbar; *l.a.*, left-auricle; *L.V.*, left ventricle; *P.A.*, pulmonary artery; *p.v.*, pulmonary vein; *p.v.c.*, posterior vena cava; *r.*, renal; *r.a.*, right auricle; *R.V.*, right ventricle; *r.v.c.*, right anterior vena cava; *Ur.*, ureter.

in a delicate tissue, the *pericardium*. The course of the veins should be followed first because they are ventral to the arteries, and the simplest plan is to trace them backwards from the auricles (Fig. 6). When they pass through muscle (flesh) this must be carefully cut away with a scalpel, or picked away with forceps.

The conspicuous arch of the aorta, curving to the

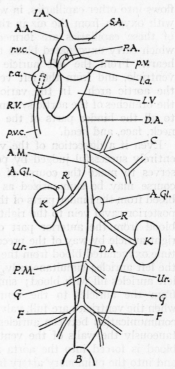

FIG. 7.—THE CHIEF POS-
TERIOR ARTERIES OF A
MAMMAL (RABBIT).

A.A., aortic arch; *A.Gl.*,
adrenal gland; *A.M.*,
anterior mesenteric; *B.*,
bladder; *C.*, cœliac;
D.A., dorsal aorta; *F.*,
femoral; *G.*, genital;
I.A., innominate; *K.*,
kidney; *l.a.*, left auricle; *L.V.*, left ventricle;
P.A., pulmonary ar-
tery; *P.M.*, posterior
mesenteric; *p.v.*, pul-
monary vein; *p.v.c.*,
posterior vena cava;
R., renal; *r.a.*, right
auricle; *R.V.*, right
ventricle; *r.v.c.*, right
anterior vena cava;
S.A., subclavian artery;
Ur., ureter.

left, is a good starting point from which to trace the arterial system (Fig. 7).

The pulmonary artery carries to the lungs *deoxy-genated* blood, which has been forced into it from the right ventricle. In the tissue of the lungs it branches into numerous capillaries. Through their thin walls

B

the blood discharges into the lungs carbon dioxide collected from all parts of the body, and this gas is expelled in respiration by way of the mouth and nose.

From the capillaries of the pulmonary artery blood flows into other capillaries, in which it becomes charged with oxygen from the air in the lungs. By the union of these capillaries are formed the *pulmonary veins*, which carry oxygenated blood to the left auricle of the heart. From the left auricle it flows into the left ventricle, and from the left ventricle it is forced into the aortic arch. In the various tissues of the body the branches of the aortic system carry *oxygenated* blood to all the hinder parts of the body and to the arms, neck, face, and head.

Even if a dissection of the veins and arteries is not entirely successful judged by professional standards, it serves to make the course of circulation clear. This course may be summarized as follows: deoxygenated blood from the hinder parts of the body passes along the posterior caval vein to the right auricle; deoxygenated blood from the anterior part of the body enters the right auricle by way of the precaval veins; at the same time oxygenated blood from the pulmonary veins enters the left auricle; simultaneously, therefore, the right and left auricles fill with blood; simultaneously blood flows from the auricles to the ventricles; simultaneously, when the ventricles are full, valves temporarily close the communication between auricles and ventricles; simultaneously the walls of the ventricles contract and the blood is forced into the aorta from the left ventricle, and into the pulmonary artery from the right ventricle.

So long as the valves of the heart are sound there is no danger of the blood making its way back to the auricles from the ventricles; it must flow onwards into the arteries. Neither can it pass backwards from the arteries to the ventricles, because the opening between ventricle and artery is also guarded by valves. These are three *semi-lunar* valves (Fig. 4), which in shape are rather like the old-fashioned watch-pockets of a four-poster bed. The hollows of these valves face the cavity of the artery, and their semi-circular closed ends are towards the ventricle. When blood is passing into the artery they lie flat against its wall. When pressure is reduced in the ventricles because their muscular contraction momentarily ceases, the blood tends to surge back along the pulmonary and aortic arteries. But, in so doing, it fills the pockets of the semi-lunar valves and stretches them across the passage-way. Strengthened protuberances from the edge of each pocket meet centrally, and the gap is most effectively closed.

An even onward flow of blood in the arteries is maintained by the entrance of more blood at each heart-beat and by the muscular action of the arterial walls.

CHAPTER III

BREATHING: THE RESPIRATORY SYSTEM

To say that respiration is the taking in of oxygen and the giving out of carbon dioxide is a very inadequate statement of this vital process. It is scarcely admissible to say that any one bodily function is more important than another, because it is on the harmonious working of the body *as a whole* that life depends. The " slow combustion " of respiration may, however, perhaps be regarded as the " key industry " of the body.

It is a matter of common knowledge that combustion, or " burning ", only takes place if there is a continuous supply of air. The explanation of this is that burning depends upon the chemical action of oxygen. This is equally true of respiration.

Air is a mixture of the gases *nitrogen* and *oxygen* in the proportion of four parts of nitrogen to one of oxygen. *Carbon dioxide* is present in varying, but always small, proportions, and there are traces of certain other gases.

When air enters the lungs of the higher animals, the hæmoglobin of the red corpuscles of the blood in the capillaries absorbs oxygen, and the unstable compound, oxyhæmoglobin, is formed. From the capillaries the blood travels along the pulmonary veins, carrying the corpuscles, with their charge of oxyhæmoglobin, to the heart. By the arterial system this oxygenated blood is distributed to all parts of the body. In the transit the oxyhæmoglobin gives up its oxygen which slowly " burns ", or " oxidizes ", parts of tissues and various storage compounds, largely carbohydrates, reducing them to simpler substances, which are transported to the heart by the caval veins (p. 29). They are then carried from the heart to the lungs by the pulmonary artery, and are finally returned to the air in the process of " breathing out ".

One of the simple products of respiration is water : when a mirror is held near the nose it is fogged with the vapour that is escaping from the lungs. Another of the breakdown products is carbon dioxide, which is carried in solution in the plasma of the blood : breathing into clear lime-water proves that this gas is set free in exhalation, for the lime-water becomes milky, and this is one of the chemical tests for the presence of carbon dioxide.

This slow combustion is not just meaningless destruction, for it is on the breaking down of complex compounds into simpler substances that the whole activity, or " energy ", of any living thing depends.

Energy can only be actively displayed if it is released from some energy store. A bag of gunpowder represents great " potent " energy—energy lying dormant, as it were. The application of a lighted match brings the potentialities into violent action. There is thus a distinction between energy that is not yet manifested, and energy that is in a state of activity. The former is known as *potential*, the latter as *kinetic*, from the Greek *kineo*, move (cf. *cinema*).

In plants and animals alike, accumulation of stores of energy depends upon feeding, which is definitely a " building-up " process, in sharp contrast with the " breaking-down " activity of respiration.

The respiratory apparatus of higher animals is a complex system. In Mammals (p. 14) air enters the body by way of the nose. As it passes along the nostrils it is moistened and warmed, so that it will neither dry nor chill the delicate tissue of the lungs when it reaches them. In the nose, too, a good deal of dust and dirt is separated from the air and held back in the nostrils, so that it cannot enter the lungs and impair their efficiency.

From the nostrils the moistened, warmed, and purified air passes to the back of the mouth, which it leaves through the *glottis;* this leads into the organ of voice, the *larynx*, which is connected with the lungs by a long, straight tube—the *trachea*, or wind-pipe (Fig. 8).

The trachea is situated in front of—that is, ventral to—the œsophagus, with which it runs parallel. Unlike the œsophagus, it always keeps its tubular form, because it is strengthened by rings of cartilage. The cartilaginous rings are incomplete dorsally, so that when the œsophagus is distended in the action of swallowing (p. 20), its wall is protected from frictional rub.

All these parts, and their relation to one another, are plainly seen in a bunch of offal, which includes heart, liver, lungs, wind-pipe, and œsophagus. The

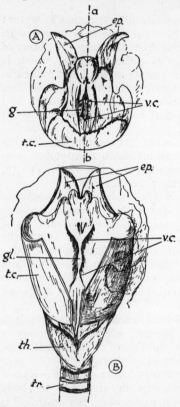

FIG. 8.—LARYNX OF OX. A, AS SEEN FROM ABOVE. B, CUT IN THE PLANE *ab* OF A.

ep., epiglottis; *g.*, glottis; *gl.*, glottal slit; *t.c.*, thyroid cartilage (Adam's apple); *v.c.*, vocal chords; *th.*, thyroid gland; *tr.*, trachea.

branching of the trachea into two *bronchi* is obvious;
if the tissue of the lungs is cut away, still finer branches
—the *bronchioles*—can be traced (Fig. 9).

The bronchioles end as " air-sacs " of microscopic
size. These are the *alveoli* of the lungs, and it is here
that the exchange of gases takes place. The alveoli
have very thin walls and are very close together. If it
were possible to spread out the air-sacs of an adult

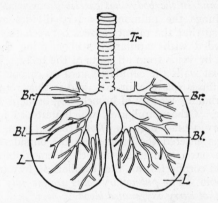

FIG. 9.—DIAGRAM OF HUMAN LUNGS.
Br., bronchus; *Bl.*, bronchiole; *L.*, lung; *Tr.*, trachea.

human being, they would cover 100 square metres.
This gives some idea of the area through which interchange of gases takes place.

Current terminology may make it a little difficult for
a beginner to grasp the details of this gaseous interchange. In the first place it must be realized that the
heart acts as a " pumping station ", and the lungs as
an " aerating station ". In the second place, it must
be remembered that arteries and veins are defined
according to their relation to the heart, irrespective of the
quality of the blood they carry: arteries carry blood

from the heart; veins carry blood *to* the heart. This is true whether the blood be oxygenated or deoxygenated.

Deoxygenated blood, with the waste products of tissue respiration, is taken to the right auricle of the heart by three caval veins. From the auricle it flows into the ventricle. From the ventricle it flows along the pulmonary artery to the lungs, *and this artery is the only one in the body that carries deoxygenated blood*. In the lungs the pulmonary artery divides and subdivides, so that the minute spaces between the air-sacs are crowded with capillaries, still carrying the waste collected by veins from all parts of the body. Through their moist walls the capillaries give up carbon dioxide, which diffuses *into* the air-sacs, and is then returned to the external air by way of bronchioles, bronchi, trachea, and nose. Other capillaries, which unite to form the pulmonary veins, take in, *from* the air-sacs, oxygen which has entered the lungs from the outside air, and which at once combines with the hæmoglobin of the red blood-corpuscles in the capillaries, forming oxy-hæmoglobin. *The pulmonary veins are the only veins in the body that carry oxygenated blood*.

By way of the pulmonary veins, the left auricle, the left ventricle, and the arterial system, oxygen is carried to all tissues of the body. It is brought into contact with every part of the tissues by *lymph*, which bathes all the cells of which the tissues are composed (p. 113). Lymph is the plasma of blood which has oozed out through the thin capillary walls.

When the arteries are carrying blood through tissues that are in a condition of " oxygen hunger ", the oxy-hæmoglobin gives up its charge of oxygen, and the gas then makes its way into the lymph-bathed cells.

The amount of fluid that bathes the tissues is controlled by thin-walled, colourless vessels called *lymphatics*, into which all excess fluid drains. The *lymphatics* open into veins at various points, and in this way the fluid they have collected is returned to the blood.

There are many bodily activities that are controlled by, and depend on, the exercise of the will : these are known as *voluntary* actions. Others, which are *involuntary*, take place quite apart from the will of the individual. The muscular action that is responsible for partly digested food passing from the stomach to the small intestine (p. 22) is purely involuntary. So, too, is the whole process of breathing, which is determined by the action of muscles that are quite beyond our control.

The involuntary character of respiration depends upon the muscular action of the arched diaphragm that separates the chest from the abdomen (p. 16). Its movement is determined by two *phrenic* nerves which extend from the neck to the diaphragm, where they branch repeatedly. The impulse they carry from the hinder part of the brain (p. 49) causes the diaphragm to lose its convexity (its concavity, if viewed from the abdominal, instead of from the thoracic side) and become flat. This change of shape automatically enlarges the cavity of the thorax. At the same time the ribs are raised by the contraction of strong muscles that lie between them, and so the chest cavity is still further enlarged. As a result of this automatic increase in space, air *must* enter. It passes inwards from the outside world to the air-sacs of the lungs, which expand to fill the extra available space. The elasticity of the lungs is partly responsible for the ejection of air, but expiration also depends upon the return of the ribs and diaphragm to their original positions.

CHAPTER IV

MOVEMENT: MUSCLES AND SKELETON

THE power of movement is a characteristic commonly associated with animals—movement of the different parts of the body, and movement of the whole body from one place to another in space.

It is true that there are some lowly animals, like *Hydra* (p. 147), that spend much of their life fixed firmly to one spot. Others, again, like *Amœba*, progress very simply by the flowing of the protoplasm of the unicellular body (p. 147).

But the vast majority of animals have a complicated mode of progression: they may crawl, fly, swim, or walk. Many can move different parts of their bodies for more than one purpose: flies use their legs for cleaning as well as for locomotion; because of its flexible neck, a bird can turn its head through a wide angle, and preen its feathers with its beak; the higher animals, more especially Man, can carry out complicated series of movements with the fore-limbs.

All such movements depend upon the harmonious co-ordination of three factors: there must be muscles on whose contraction and expansion all movement depends; there must be something firm to which the muscle is attached, so that it gets a " pull "; in connection with every muscle there must be nerves which initiate, regulate, and control all muscular action.

The necessary support is provided by a *skeleton*. This is a firm structure to which muscles are attached and which determines both the shape and movements of the body; it also protects the more delicate bodily organs from injury.

In many of the lower animals—in Wood-lice, Beetles, Lobsters, and so on—the supporting framework is an *exo*skeleton (Greek, *exo*, outside). Fishes have an exoskeleton of scales, but also an *endo*skeleton of cartilage or bone.

In all Mammals the skeleton, which is composed of bone, is internal and is highly developed (Fig. 10).

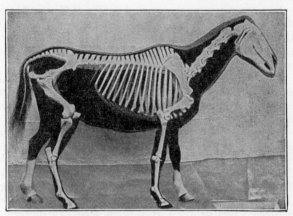

FIG. 10.—SKELETON OF HORSE.   [*Bastin.*

This bony framework must not be rigid, for that would reduce the power of movement to a minimum. To give flexibility the bones of the body move one upon another forming joints, of which there are more than 200 in the body of Man.

In spite of this large number of joints, there is normally no creaking when they are at work—as one writes, for instance, nothing more than the scratch of the pen is heard. Friction is avoided, partly because there is a thin sheet of cartilage (gristle) over the ends of the bones, and partly because all joints are bathed in the lubricating *synovial* fluid, which makes easy movement possible. When a joint is injured there is often an increased output of the fluid. Synovitis, or " water on the knee," is common when a knee has been " put out of joint ". With increasing age the synovial fluid is not so readily produced and, as a result, the easy movements of youth are lost, and creaking of the stiffened joints often accompanies movement.

In most museums there are skeletons of Man and other Mammals and it is clear, on examination, that they are all based on one fundamental plan. Each has a long axis—the " backbone " or *spine*—which supports two pairs of limbs laterally and the skull terminally.

Part of the skull—the *cranium*—is hollow and, in life, encloses and protects the brain. The other parts are the *nasal apparatus* and the *jaws*, which together make up the *face*.

In a young skeleton the skull is seen to be made up of several bones, with irregular margins that dove-tail into one another in a zigzag way. In older animals the zigzagging has disappeared, and it is not easy to distinguish the boundaries of the different bones. In human beings this obliteration has generally taken place at about eighteen years of age. It was on such evidence that, by means of X-ray photographs, it was possible to determine the youth of Tutankhamen.

Here and there in a skull there are small, roundish gaps between the bones ; in life it is through these that nerves pass outward from the brain to different parts of the body.

The spine is made up of separate bones called *vertebræ* (Lat. *vertere*, to turn) which " turn ", or move, one upon another, making it possible for the body to bend forwards and backwards, and turn from side to side.

Structural details of the vertebræ differ in different regions of the spine, but all agree in general plan. The vertebræ are hollow, and within the long tube, produced by their end-to-end arrangement, the *spinal cord* is lodged and protected. Each vertebra has certain convexities and concavities which articulate with the concavities and convexities of the vertebræ that meet it at either end, and so make movement, one upon another, possible. From all vertebræ, except those at the end of the tail, *transverse processes* of flattened bone project and serve for the attachment of muscles.

When a rabbit is stewed the vertebræ generally separate, and if they are collected and washed the whole spinal column can be reconstructed. It is a good plan to thread them, in order, on a piece of coarse twine.

In the neck of a mammal there are seven *cervical* vertebræ. Even in the enormously long neck of a Giraffe there are only seven, and the number is the same in the extremely short neck of the Whale.

The first of the cervical vertebræ is the *atlas*, which supports the skull in such a way that the head can nod. It is the articulation of the second vertebra, the *axis*, that makes it possible for the head to turn.

In the chest region there are generally twelve *thoracic* vertebræ, but sometimes there are thirteen. It is with these vertebræ that the ribs articulate. The thoracic vertebræ have very long spines which slope backwards in the first nine bones.

Posterior to the thoracics are the *lumbars*. Whether there are seven or six of these depends upon the number of the thoracic vertebræ.

Posterior to the lumbars are fused vertebræ forming the *sacrum*, and lastly there are the *caudal* vertebræ which, at the end of the tail, are merely tiny, solid bones.

The two pairs of limbs are connected with the axis by means of " girdles ". That of the chest region—the *pectoral* girdle—only incompletely encircles the spine. The other, at the base of the lumbar region, is complete, and much more rigid, for its bones are more firmly united : this is the *pelvic* girdle.

The largest bones of the pectoral girdle are the *scapulas*, or shoulder-blades, whose triangular shape is familiar to everyone who has carved a shoulder of mutton. A prominent ridge runs the whole length of the shoulder-blade; strong muscles which are attached to both sides of this give the arm and shoulder-blade their range of movement. These muscles are carved into slices when the lean meat of a shoulder of mutton is cut. Near the bone the muscle gives place to a tough, shiny substance which is the *tendon* that attaches the muscle to the bone.

The remaining part of this limb-girdle is formed by the *clavicles*, or collar-bones, which are very small in the rabbit. As the chief use of the clavicle is to help to support the arms, it is most strongly developed in animals whose fore-limbs carry out a wide range of movement. It is absent in Donkeys, Cows and Horses, which use their fore-limbs only for locomotion; as Dogs, Rabbits, and Cats, for instance, use these limbs in various operations, they have a small clavicle; the fore-limbs of Birds are the much-used wings, and their clavicle is the comparatively large " merry thought"; in ourselves it is much more strongly developed than in other animals, because we do so much more work with the fore-limbs of the body.

Into the groove at the apex of the shoulder-blade fits the rounded head of the *humerus*. This is the long bone of the arm that extends from shoulder to elbow, where its meeting with the two bones of the fore-arm forms the elbow joint. These two bones are the *ulna* and *radius*. At the " funny-bone" end the ulna has a pronounced groove for articulation with the humerus. The radius, which leads directly to the thumb, is a shorter bone and, in Man, " radiates " over the ulna, thus making it possible for the arm to be used in many ways. If the right arm, with the palm of the hand facing upwards, is held by the left hand midway between wrist and elbow, the rotation of radius on ulna is felt when the hand is turned to make the palm face inwards and downwards.

The wrist-bones meet the level ends of ulna and radius and support the hand.

The plan of the hind-limb closely resembles that of the fore-limb. The long thigh-bone, or *femur*, has a prominent, rounded head that fits closely into a roundish hollow at the side of the pelvic girdle. At its farther end it articulates with two bones which are very unequal in size ; the *tibia* and the *fibula*. In the Rabbit the small, fragile fibula fuses with the tibia, which in this case is the longest bone of the body ; in Man the fibula is a separate bone extending from the knee to the foot, where it forms the lump on the outer side of the ankle. The ankle is made up of small bones, similar to those of the wrist. At the knee, where the femur articulates with the tibia, there is a protecting " knee-cap ". When the knee bends, the " cap " slides in a deep groove on the front face of the thigh-bone.

In all vertebrates higher than the Fishes, whose girdles support paired fins, it is characteristic for the limbs to end in five digits, either fingers or toes; they are therefore known as *pentadactyl*. In such a limb one long bone articulates with two separate bones, which in their turn, articulate with the small bones of wrist or ankle ; these support the bones of the palm of the hand and the sole of the foot, beyond which are the five digits.

From such a ground-plan have been derived the variations characteristic of the limbs of Amphibia, Reptiles, Birds, and Mammals. These variations are manifold. In the Rabbit the articulation of the radius and ulna is such that they cannot move one upon the other ; the tibia and fibula are fused; the hind paw has only four digits. In the Horse only one perfect toe remains. In Birds the fore-limb is modified to form a wing ; there is great reduction in the bones of hand and wrist ; the thumb and second finger are each represented by one bone only, instead of having two and three respectively; the first finger has two instead of three joints, and of the other two digits there is no trace. In Frogs the radius and ulna are completely fused; the only indication of their dual character is a groove along the length of the bone.

CHAPTER V

MENTAL ACTIVITY: THE NERVOUS SYSTEM

IN very early embryonic life every vertebrate animal develops *dorsal nerve tissue* which, at the forward end of the body, expands, forming three hollow, bulb-like swellings—the *fore-brain*, the *mid-brain*, and the *hind-brain*. The degree of intelligence of different classes of vertebrates depends on the further development of these three original expansions.

The fore-brain gives rise to the *cerebrum*, or *cerebral hemispheres*. The *optic lobes* develop from the mid-brain. From the hind-brain develop the *cerebellum* and the *medulla oblongata* (Fig. 11).

Intelligence depends much more upon the convolutions of the brain than upon its size. The whole bulk of the brain is not concerned with thought, which is restricted to the cerebral hemispheres. Even in this limited region it is only upon the *cerebral cortex*, or "grey matter", that the power of thinking depends. In Man this outer layer is not more than $\frac{1}{9}$ inch thick, but it is made up of some 9,000,000,000 cells.

Obviously the greater the number of the cerebral convolutions, and the deeper the grooves between them, the greater is the area of the cortex, and the more extensive, therefore, is the region concerned with the higher mental activities.

The cerebral hemispheres are the centre of all actions that depend upon will, intelligence, and feeling. In Mammals they are so large that they extend backwards over the rest of the brain. This extension is most pronounced in the human race.

The hind-brain controls many *reflex*, or *involuntary*,

actions—as, for instance, breathing, swallowing, and the beating of the heart.

Because of its ceaseless work, the brain needs an unfailing supply of food and oxygen. The blood-vessels that bring these to the brain and those that carry away waste matter are in an extremely thin tissue—the

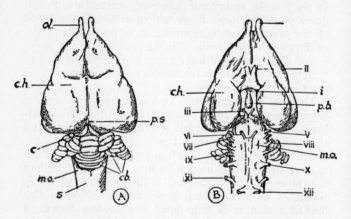

FIG. 11.—THE BRAIN OF THE RABBIT. A, DORSAL SURFACE. B, VENTRAL SURFACE. THE NUMERALS REFER TO THE PAIRED CRANIAL NERVES.

c., optic lobes; *cb.*, cerebellum; *c.h.*, cerebral hemisphere; *i.*, the infundibulum that bears *p.b.*, the pituitary gland; *m.o.*, medulla oblongata; *ol.*, olfactory lobe; *s.*, spinal cord; *p.s.*, stalk of pineal gland.

pia mater—which over-lies the cerebral cortex and closely follows all the convolutions of the cerebral hemispheres. A thicker tissue—the *dura mater*—forms the outermost covering of the brain, and between this and the *pia mater* is the delicate *arachnoid membrane*. These three tissue-layers are the *meninges* of the brain. Inflammation of these tissues leads to a great increase in the amount of lymph (p. 40) normally present between the layers, and is the cause of meningitis.

Every living part of the body has some particular work to do. For this it is not enough that the part concerned be well supplied with food and oxygen. In addition, it must receive some incitement to activity, and it is the work of the nervous system to transmit the necessary stimuli. From the brain and the spinal cord, which comprise the *central nervous system*, arise paired nerves, whose delicate ramifications " innervate " definite muscles in the various parts of the body.

It is the special work of some of these nerves to carry messages *inwards* to the central nervous system; these are *sensory*, or *afferent*, nerves. Others conduct impulses *outwards* to the muscles, which then make appropriate reactions; these are the *motor*, or *efferent*, nerves.

Because every nerve is a bundle of fibres it may be *mixed*, some of its fibres carrying sense-impressions inwards, while others are motor and either incite, or inhibit, muscular action.

Impulses carried by motor-nerves may cause muscles to act *involuntarily*, without the will of the individual. Such involuntary, or *reflex*, actions are illustrated by the beating of the heart; by the passing of partly digested food at intervals from stomach to intestine; by the whole muscular movement of respiration; by the uncontrolled start that follows the loud noise of an explosion.

Control of *voluntary* action, on the other hand, depends upon the will of the individual. It is illustrated by the hesitations and decisions of any one of us at a pedestrian crossing—the turning of the head to the right and left, the preliminary forward motion, the drawing back, the final crossing, and the muscular relaxation which follows when the opposite kerb is reached. In this output of energy between 300 and 400 muscles are brought into play, all regulated by a still higher number of the fine endings of nerves controlled by the central nervous system.

In the complicated action of crossing a busy street, sensory nerves are stimulated by sight and sound. They carry a message to certain groups of cells in the brain; from these a message is transmitted to neighbouring groups that, in their turn, transmit the message along motor-nerves to the particular muscles that make the appropriate response.

This explanation of the reception and transmission of stimuli takes some seconds to write or read. But when the thumb and fingers, for instance, are burned by a lighted match, only a flash of time is needed for sensory nerves to carry the message to the brain; for the necessary communications to be made in the brain-tissue; for the message to travel to the finger tips along the motor-nerves; for the muscles they innervate to relax; and for the match-end to be dropped.

It is a difficult matter to examine the brain of a rabbit in detail, because it is almost certain to be injured when the hard bone of the cranium is chipped away. It is, however, worth while to remove enough bone to expose a part, at least, of the brain. This operation must be prepared for on the day the rabbit is received because brain-tissue degenerates very quickly after death. If a small hole is made in the skull some of the formalin in which the rabbit is kept will pass into the cranium and will harden, as well as preserve, the delicate tissue of the brain.

In Mammals twelve pairs of nerves branch laterally from the brain, as shown in Fig. 11.

1. The *olfactory* nerves convey sensations of smell.

2. The *optic* nerves are responsible for sight.

3, 4, 6. These three pairs are motor-nerves and control the muscles on which movements of the eyes depend.

5. The fifth pair, whose branches are distributed to the mouth and face generally, are mixed nerves. We can trace the course of their sensory fibres in toothache and neuralgia. Their motor-fibres control the muscles concerned in chewing.

7. Facial expression depends upon the seventh pair of nerves, which control our smiles, frowns, and the like.

8. It is on the eighth pair of nerves that hearing depends.

9. The ninth pair are distributed to the tongue and the back of the mouth, and are concerned with the sensation of taste.

10. The nerves of the tenth pair are very long. Their branches extend to the larynx, heart, lungs, liver, and alimentary tract. Because of its " wandering ", the tenth nerve is called the *vagus*.

11, 12. The eleventh pair of nerves innervate the muscles of the neck, and the twelfth those of the tongue.

From the spinal cord pairs of spinal nerves pass out between the vertebræ, and are in connection with all parts of the body to which the cranial nerves do not extend.

In addition to the central nervous system, there is another system of nerves, known as the *sympathetic*. Two main trunks, one on each side of the spine, give off branches which innervate muscles of the visceral organs; other delicate ramifications meet corresponding branches of the spinal cord. In the abdomen, near the diaphragm, part of the sympathetic system has been given the fanciful name of " solar plexus " because of its many radiating fibres. It is on account of this plexus that a blow " below the belt " may have very serious consequences.

The multitude of *touch* impressions, that are the

predominant sensations of our early life, are received by nerves whose delicate branches occur all over the body below the epidermis. Impressions of contact in the legs, arms, and body generally, are carried to the spinal cord by way of the sensory fibres of spinal nerves. In the head and face region they reach the brain by way of sensory fibres of cranial nerves.

The senses of *taste* and *smell* are so intimately con-

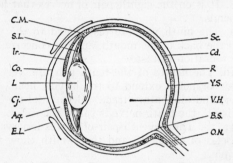

FIG. 12.—DIAGRAM OF THE EYE.

Aq., aqueous chamber; *B.S.*, blind spot; *Cd.*, choroid; *C.M.*, muscle; *Co.*, cornea; *E.L.*, eyelid; *Cj.*, conjunctiva; *Ir.*, iris; *L.*, lens; *O.N.*, optic nerve; *R.*, retina; *Sc.*, sclerotic; *S.L.*, suspensory ligament; *V.H.*, vitreous humour; *Y.S.*, yellow spot.

nected that it is not easy to distinguish one from the other. Many sensations commonly regarded as taste are really sensations of smell. Both depend upon tactile impressions received by nerve-endings below the epidermis of tongue and nostrils respectively. The intimate relation between these senses is experienced when olfactory sensations are blunted during a bad cold and food " loses its taste ". For the same reason the unpleasantness of taking a nasty medicine is greatly modified if the nose is tightly nipped.

For the most part tactile impressions are vague and

diffuse. For more exact recording more delicate and specialized receiving apparatus is essential, and this is found in the eye and the ear.

The eye (Fig. 12) is protected by the bony socket in which it rests, and is held in place by three pairs of muscles and by the optic nerve.

It is bounded by a three-layered wall, of which the outermost layer—the *sclerotic*—is thick, tough, and opaque, except at the front of the eye where rays of light must pass through the wall. The *choroid*, which underlies the sclerotic, contains dark pigment which, like the black lining of a camera, prevents light that has once entered from being reflected outwards. The choroid does not pass over the front of the eye, but ends as a muscular ring—the *iris*. The *pupil* of the eye is the opening of this ring, whose muscles control the size of the pupil so that, as in the similar mechanism of the stops of a camera, the aperture is either increased or diminished, and the amount of light that enters the eye is thus regulated. The innermost layer of the three-layered wall is the *retina*.

By dissecting a large eye, such as that of an ox, a great deal of its structure is made clear.

The *lens* is found behind the iris, blocking the hole, or pupil. It is held in position by an enfolding tissue attached to the choroid and called the *suspensory ligament*. In front of the lens is a small chamber which contains a watery fluid (*aqueous humour*). The larger chamber behind the lens contains *vitreous humour*, which is of a rather glassy, gelatinous nature. This chamber is lined by the retina, which is the actual sensory region of the eye. Its cells are the final branches of the optic nerve; they are of two kinds known as " rods " and " cones ", and probably carry out different functions. Everyone knows how difficult it is to match colours by artificial light. A suggested explanation of this is that in the daylight we judge colour by the cones only, but that in artificial light the rods also take part in the process.

Rays of light that enter the eye are directed to, and focused upon, the retina by the lens. Muscles connected with the suspensory ligament relax at need so that it loosens a little. Because the lens is somewhat elastic it can become more, or less, convex, as the suspensory ligament is loose or taut. It is this accommodation of the lens that enables the eye to focus objects at different distances. The sense impressions received by the retina are carried to the brain by the optic nerve, and the individual " sees ". In failing sight the eye does not focus properly because the lens is not becoming sufficiently convex; spectacles with convex lenses must then be worn for close work.

Impressions of sound, like those of sight, are received by a highly specialized sensory area.

In our ears there are three distinct parts : the external, the middle, and the inner ear (Fig. 13).

The flap of the ear, or *pinna*, is characteristic of Mammals. The majority of human beings have lost the power of moving the flap, which is definitely of service to animals such as Dogs, Horses, and Rabbits, which " prick up " their ears to receive waves of sound.

From the pinna a tube passes to the *middle ear*, which is protected by a rounded, prominent bone behind the pinna. The middle ear is the " drum ", or *tympanum*. It is a cavity containing air, and is shut off from the tube of the external ear by a tightly stretched drum-membrane. On the far side of the drum, opposite this *tympanic membrane*, a small gap in the wall is closed by a thin layer of cartilage known as the " oval window ". Stretching across the drum, from the tympanic membrane to the oval window, there is a chain of small bones —the *auditory ossicles*.

The parts of the ear so far described are not present in all vertebrates. In Reptiles and Birds the external ear is merely the tube that leads to the drum-membrane; there is no flap surrounding the external opening. In Amphibians there is no tube, and the drum-membrane is flush with the skin of the head; it is seen as a darker

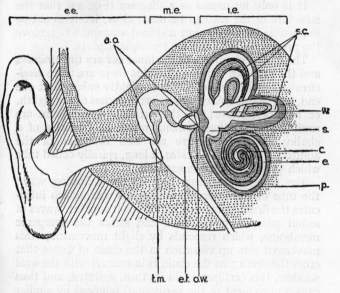

FIG. 13.—DIAGRAM OF HUMAN EAR.

a.o., auditory ossicles; *c.*, cochlea; *e.*, endolymph; *e.e.*, external ear; *e.t.*, Eustachian tube; *i.e.*, internal ear; *m.e.*, middle ear; *o.w.*, oval window; *p.*, perilymph; *s.*, sacculus; *s.c.*, semi-circular canals; *t.m.*, tympanic membrane; *w.*, utriculus.

patch of skin just behind the eye of a Frog; in Amphibians, too, only one bone stretches across the drum-cavity. In Fishes all the parts of the ear so far described are absent.

It is the *inner ear* that is actually concerned with hearing. It is so complicated that it is called the

" membraneous labyrinth ". Its delicate structures are protected from the bone in which they are enclosed, by being surrounded with *peri*lymph. All the channels of the internal ear contain a similar fluid—the *endo*lymph.

It is only by means of a diagram (Fig. 13) that the structure of the ear can be made clear, for it would be impossible for anyone but a skilled anatomist to remove the protecting bone and see the various parts.

The largest chambers of the inner ear are the *utriculus* and the *sacculus*. In the utriculus there are three *semi-circular canals*, each of which is slightly enlarged at one end, and to this enlargement pass branches of the eighth, or auditory, nerve; in the utriculus itself there are similar nerve-endings, among which lie particles of a chalky substance. There are also branches of the auditory nerve in the *cochlea*, a long, spirally coiled tube which projects from the sacculus.

The whole mechanism acts in the following way: the tube of the external ear secretes wax, which lubricates the drum-membrane and keeps it supple; waves of sound pass down the tube and strike the tympanic membrane, which responds by slight movement; this movement sets up vibration in the chain of bones that cross the drum; as the chain is in contact with the oval window, this cartilage is, in its turn, agitated, and thus causes movement of the perilymph, followed by similar movement of the endolymph within the channels of the inner ear; but in and around these channels are delicate branches of the auditory nerve, and they receive the sound-impressions, which are then transmitted along the auditory nerve to the brain.

Various theories have been put forward to account for the actual " hearing ". The one most generally accepted is a modification of the Helmholtz Piano Theory. When the strings of a piano are exposed, some of them are seen to vibrate when certain notes are sung. In the cochlea of the inner ear an extremely delicate, spirally coiled ribbon is attached along one edge. It is made up of about 24,000 elastic fibres that gradually decrease in length. The piano-theory states that, as a result of air-vibrations, or waves, each fibre responds to a certain tone, the longer fibres vibrating to the deeper notes.

While the cochlea of the internal ear receives sound-impressions, it is the utriculus and its semicircular canals that help the body to keep its balance. When the head is moved the fragments of chalky substance change their position and press upon different cells. In this way different parts of the nerve-endings are stimulated, and different " position sensations " are experienced by the individual. If one spins round rapidly, then suddenly stops, there is a feeling of giddiness and of spinning in the opposite direction—the room " goes round ". The giddy feeling may last for 30 seconds or more because, during this time, the fluid in the semicircular canals is, apparently, continuing to spin, although the head itself is still.

CHAPTER VI

GLANDS: THEIR VITAL IMPORTANCE

A GLAND, as was evident from the work of the *pancreas*
(p. 17), produces some particular substance to carry
out some particular work.

The largest gland in the body is the *liver*. It produces bile that is carried by the bile-duct to the small
intestine, where, like the secretions of the pancreas, it
aids digestion. The liver is two-lobed, each lobe being
incompletely divided into two (Fig. 1). Near the dividing line of the two lobes, but actually embedded in that
of the right side, is the *gall-bladder*. It is difficult to
say of what use this is to the body, for in some Mammals
—in the Horse, for instance—it is not present. It is
too small to be regarded as a storing-place for bile, for
in Man it can hold, at most, only about one ounce, and
the daily flow of bile in a human being is 500–800 c.c.
If, however, the bile is prevented from passing through
the gall-bladder of Man, it is absorbed by the blood,
and jaundice results.

Apart from acting as a gland, the liver carries out
other work of great importance :—

1. *It acts as a storehouse for digested food.* Digested
food is carried to the liver from the small intestine by
the portal vein (p. 23). When it is needed it leaves
the liver by way of the *hepatic* veins, and is then distributed to those parts of the body that are in need of
nutrition.

2. *It regulates the amount of sugar in the blood.* It is
essential that there should be a constant, though somewhat low, percentage of sugar in the blood. If there
were no control there would be too much sugar after a

meal; the excess would be got rid of by the kidneys; a period would follow in which the blood was deficient in sugar, and the tissues would consequently be deprived of this food. To prevent such fluctuation the liver stores the surplus in the form of *glycogen*; this is converted into sugar (*glucose*), and passed into the bloodstream at need, to make good the loss due to sugar-absorption by the tissues. It is the presence of glucose that accounts for the sweet taste of the liver we eat.

3. *The liver prepares nitrogenous waste* which is carried to the kidneys by the blood. In the kidneys urea is separated from the blood and passes along special tubes—the *ureters* (Fig. 6)—to the bladder, from which it is periodically discharged.

The kidneys cannot be considered as glands, because they do not actually prepare, but merely extract, the liquid that they discharge. They are seen in the rabbit lying one on either side of the vertebral column; the right kidney has a more forward position in the body than the left (Fig. 6). The whole kidney is a mass of tubes of very small diameter. In a half-kidney it is seen that the outer region differs from the inner. In the outer region the tubules do not follow a straight course; they are here extracting water, urea, and other waste substances from blood brought to them by special capillaries. In the central part of the kidney the tubules run straight, carrying the waste to the ureter, along which it passes to the bladder.

Near each kidney, as can be seen in the partly dissected rabbit, there is a round, yellowish body, which is an *adrenal* gland (Fig. 6). The secretion of these glands is produced in excess in strong emotion, such as love, fear, and anger. As the result of a sudden shock the secretion is arrested, producing definite effects in the individual: the flesh " creeps " because blood is diverted from vessels below the skin; hair " stands on end " (as is well seen in a cat defying a dog) because muscles in connection with each hair-follicle contract and give the hair an upright pull.

In addition to that discharged from the kidneys, liquid waste is also eliminated by way of the skin. Under normal conditions about 700 c.c. of sweat are evaporated from our bodies every 24 hours. This waste, which is secreted by sweat-glands in the skin, passes along narrow ducts and escapes through pores at the surface. As well as ridding the body of waste, sweat also helps to regulate the temperature of the body. As a result of oxidation in every living cell (p 40), all tissues give heat to the body, and this would become excessive if it were not reduced in some way. The evaporation of sweat from the skin is one way in which heat is drawn from the body, because temperature is lowered in evaporation. (This is the principle of the cheap, porous butter-coolers that are now so much used in hot weather.) Dogs have sweat-glands only in the skin between their toes, and this is why they pant, open-mouthed, when they are very hot : the excessive respiratory movements remove heat by way of the lungs and, also, evaporation is taking place from the tongue and mouth.

In a dissected rabbit the *thymus* gland can be seen overlying the heart. This, like the adrenals, is one of the *endocrine*, or " ductless ", glands; that is it discharges its secretion directly into the blood without the intervention of a duct, such as the bile-duct of the liver and the narrow ducts that conduct sweat to the pores of the skin. The function of the thymus is obscure, but probably, to some extent, it controls development before birth. Normally this gland disappears in adult man. In abnormal cases where it persists a sudden shock may have unexpected, even fatal, results.

Other ductless glands are the minute *pituitary* and *pineal* bodies. The former (Fig. 11B) is on the ventral surface of the brain. If there is deficiency in its secretion, growth in height is checked and abnormal fatness results; excess of secretion causes greatly exaggerated growth in the bones of hands and feet and of the lower jaw.

The secretions of the pineal body, which is on the dorsal surface of the brain (Fig. 11A), apparently influence the development of the *reproductive organs* (p. 66), which may also be regarded as ductless glands. Apart from the fact that the *ovaries* produce eggs and the *testes* produce sperms, they give out secretions which have marked effects on widely separated parts of the body. They influence, for instance, the growth of hair; changes in the *timbre* of the voice; the growth, in certain Mammals, of horns, antlers, mane, and so on.

The *thyroid* (Fig. 8), a most important ductless gland, is seen more satisfactorily in a bunch of offal than in the rabbit's body. It consists of reddish, flattened lobes which lie one on each side of the larynx. The thyroid secretes *thyroxin*, which contains 65 per cent. of iodine. In young children deficiency of the secretion causes stunted growth and arrested mental development. In adults a deficiency induces myxœdema, a disease in which an individual becomes fat and dull, the hair falls out, and the skin is dry and coarse. Treatment in this case consists in giving thyroid secretion extracted from the glands of lower animals, usually sheep. When the secretion is in excess, the gland and the neck swell and the eyes protrude. Irritability and general lack of nervous control are symptoms of this condition.

The thyroid gland is attached to the thyroid cartilage (Fig. 8), which encloses the larynx on three sides. In the human race this cartilage is much more prominent in man than in woman, and is popularly known as " Adam's apple ". If the larynx in the bunch of offal is cut longitudinally, two strips of tissue are seen stretching across it. These are the "vocal chords" (Fig. 8.) Air passing over them causes vibration in the so-called "chords" and produces sound in much the same way as in the reed-vibrations of an organ-pipe, or as in the vibration of a blade of grass that is blown when firmly held between the thumbs.

The *spleen*, which is not actually a gland, lies behind the stomach in the rabbit, being attached to it at the end nearest the œsophagus. In it red corpuscles are destroyed and white corpuscles multiply.

Tonsils are at the back of the soft palate, one on either side. It is difficult to say what their function is. They often become diseased and cause various ear and throat troubles. On the other hand, they are active centres for the production of those white blood corpuscles that defend the body against bacterial attack, and it may be, therefore, that they give protection against "germs".

The internal secretions of glands contain the *hormones*, or "chemical messengers", which influence to an incalculable degree the activity, or "behaviour", of all living things. These substances, which are produced in very small quantities in one organ, stimulate the activities of other organs, especially those of secretion; they are carried in the blood-stream from the organ in which they are produced to that in which the reaction takes place. It has been said that if, in Man, "all the glands of internal secretions were rolled together, they would form a parcel small enough to go into a waistcoat pocket, yet such a small mass can influence the working and growth of the whole body".

With special reference to the secretion of the adrenal glands Sir Arthur Thomson writes: "The influence of mind on body finds a good illustration in the stimulation of the adrenal glands by strong emotion. Increase in the powerful 'chemical messenger', or hormone, which the blood sweeps away, has numerous effects through the body. It constricts the blood-vessels and there is less blood in the peripheral and more in the deeper parts. It raises the blood-pressure, excites and freshens the muscles, adds to the sugar-content of the blood, increases the coagulability of the blood, and so on. In short, the whole body is prepared for a fight, and all under the influence of what was to begin with a psychical event."

Another scientist writes: " Nervous control is now considered to be of a chemical nature." It is, apparently, the hormones of the secretions of the various endocrine glands that play so important a part in determining and controlling nervous response.

CHAPTER VII

REPRODUCTION: CONTINUATION OF THE RACE

As immortality is an impossibility, every individual, high or lowly, animal or plant, is so designed that it may complete its life-history by giving rise to new individuals of its own pattern.

In the simplest living things the new individuals may arise by division of the parent into two or more parts (p. 162). This is one method of *asexual reproduction*. In all plants and animals, however, that have reached any degree of complexity, and, indeed, in many that consist of one cell only, *sexual reproduction* is the rule.

In sexual reproduction nuclei of cells (p. 115) from different individuals, and therefore each with a different line of descent, unite and fuse to form one cell, which is the first stage in the development of the offspring. The cells that unite in the sexual act are named *gametes*, from the Greek, *gameo*, I marry.

The gametes of higher animals can be distinguished as male and female. Speaking generally, the male gamete is small and moves actively, while the female is larger and motionless. The female gametes, or *ova* (Lat. *ovum*, an egg), are produced by the division of cells in a special organ called an *ovary*. Cell-division inside a *testis* gives rise to the small male gametes, or *sperms*.

The fusion of a sperm with an ovum is known as *fertilization*, and gives rise to a new individual, or *embryo*.

In all Mammals but the lowest the young develop within the mother ; by her body they are protected ; from her blood they receive both food for growth and oxygen for breathing ; into her veins are passed the waste materials that result during embryonic growth. It is to this close pre-natal connection, throughout a considerable period of time, that the development of " family life " is due, which reaches its culmination in the families of the human race.

It is not difficult to trace the parts of the reproductive system in the rabbit that has been preserved in the formalin bath (Fig. 1). If it is a female it is well to find the ovaries first. They are small, yellowish-white, oval bodies attached to the dorsal wall of the abdomen and lie, one right and one left of the spinal cord, a little behind the kidneys. When they have been located, the tissue surrounding them must be carefully removed.

In close proximity with each ovary there is the opening of a tube called the *oviduct*, because along it pass the eggs (*ova*). A blunt instrument—the end of a slender skewer, for instance—can be passed into the mouth of the oviduct; but what cannot be demonstrated is, that the mouth is fringed with very fine threads of protoplasm, called *cilia*. When the eggs are ready for fertilization, they pass from the ovary into the abdominal cavity, and are drawn to the opening of the oviduct by rhythmic movements of the cilia. Having entered the tube, they pass along it, and are met and fertilized by the sperms, which have been injected into the body of the female by the *penis* of the male. The oviducts are somewhat coiled, but it is easy to trace them backward and see how they widen and expand into the *uterus*, or womb. In the uterus the fertilized eggs develop. A few days after fertilization has taken place, there is actual organic connection between each developing embryo and the uterus wall. The tissue that forms the connection is the *placenta*, and it is through the blood-capillaries of this tissue that food in solution, and oxygen for respiration, pass from the parent to the offspring.

In a male rabbit the testes, as would be expected, originate in the abdominal cavity. In the Rabbit, and many other Mammals, they are finally drawn backwards and downwards in the body and occupy two pouches of skin between the hind limbs, one on either side of the penis.

When a testis is withdrawn from the pouch in which it lies, it is seen to be a mass of much-coiled tubules. In these the sperms originate. The sperms, which have a " head " and a " tail ", are extremely minute, the head being 0·005 mm. in length and the tail 0·045 mm. It is by means of the tail that sperms swim up the fluid in the oviducts of the female and so come in contact with the eggs. The period of *gestation*, that is the time that elapses between the union of gametes and the actual birth of the young animal, is very different in different mammals, as the following instances show :—

Cat, Dog	8–9 weeks.
Lion	16 ,,
Tiger	22 ,,
Sheep	5 months.
Man, Cow	9 ,,
Horse	11 ,,
Elephant	20 months–2 years.

Thirty days elapse between the fertilization of an ovum and the birth of the rabbit into which the fertilized egg develops. When they leave the uterus the young animals are fully formed; they cannot, however, see as yet, and their hairy covering is incomplete. For some time they are dependent upon the mother for food which, in the form of milk, is supplied by the mammary glands.

SECTION II

THE PLANT AS A MACHINE INCESSANTLY AT WORK

CHAPTER VIII

FEEDING

In the chapter on evolution it is suggested that animals and plants have a common ancestor. It is only to be expected, therefore, that even to-day there should be certain resemblances between them. Except in the case of some few very simple organisms, all *external* resemblance is definitely lost, but the members of the two kingdoms still agree in so far as they carry out the same functions in the business of living—they feed, breathe, grow, respond to stimuli, and multiply on the face of the earth.

The actual way in which plants feed, however, is fundamentally different from the feeding process of animals. Plants, with some exceptions, build up their own food, using, in the manufacturing process, water, mineral salts, and carbon dioxide. They absorb the salts in solution from the soil or from the water of their habitat. They take carbon dioxide from the atmosphere, or from air dissolved in the water in which they live. Animals have no power of manufacturing food and are entirely dependent upon plants for their supplies. If, therefore, the " green things of the earth " died out, all life in the world would automatically end.

In this physiological difference lies the explanation of the fact that, generally speaking, plants are fixed in their habitat, whereas animals roam in search of food.

The ability of plants to obtain mineral salts depends upon *osmosis*. This is a process in which two liquids of different density, separated by a permeable membrane, have a mutual attraction for one another, the stronger exerting the more powerful pull.

If a thistle-funnel is handy, the attraction of a sugar solution for water can be readily demonstrated. A

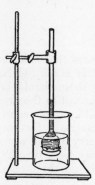

piece of pig's bladder or parchment must be tied tightly over the open end of the bulb of the funnel. The sugar solution is then poured down the tube until the bulb is full. In doing this the tube should be held in a slanting position, so that air may escape along the upper half of the tube as the syrup flows down the lower side.

The thistle-funnel is fixed so that its bulb is suspended in water in a glass (Fig. 14). In a short time liquid rises up the stem. Obviously water has passed in through the membrane, having been attracted by the dense solution in the bulb. After a time the water in the glass tastes slightly sweet,

FIG. 14.—EXPERI-
MENT TO SHOW
OSMOSIS.

because some of the sugar solution has passed outwards. The experiment can be varied by using other solutions —of salt or copper sulphate, for instance—and by reversing the liquids, so that water is in the thistle-funnel and the denser liquid in the glass.

In this experiment osmotic action is evident in non-living apparatus, and therefore no proof is given that it takes place in *living* cells. This may be demonstrated by using a large potato instead of a thistle-funnel. With the exception of the outside skin, a potato is entirely made up of living cells.

Two potatoes are used in the experiment, for one acts as a control. A small slice is cut off the end of each so that it stands on a flat base. As liquids cannot penetrate the corky skin, a narrow ring of this is peeled away at the base. Down the middle of each potato a pit is bored, stopping short within half an inch of the base. The potatoes are now put into a dish containing water to the depth of one inch (Fig. 15).

The pit of one potato is left empty, and this is the control which serves for comparison. Into the other is put a little sugar, which dissolves in the moisture that escapes from the cut cells, forming a sugar solution at the bottom of the pit. There is a rise in the level of the liquid here, as in the glass tube of the thistle-funnel. The solution first attracts water from the cells lining the pit; because of the loss of

FIG. 15.—EXPERIMENT TO DE-MONSTRATE OSMOSIS IN LIV-ING CELLS.

water, the sap in these particular cells becomes stronger, so that it, in its turn, attracts water from neighbouring cells farther away from the pit; the sap of these cells therefore becomes stronger and exerts attraction; in this way a movement of water is started which ultimately affects the cells on the outside of the potato so that they, in their turn, attract water from the dish in which the potato stands. In quite a short time so much water rises in the pit that it overflows and trickles down the outside of the potato. In the control experiment there has been no such rise, and the pit is quite dry.

In the higher plants it is through the very delicate *root-hairs* that solutions are absorbed from the soil (Fig. 16). The osmotic solutions are the cell-sap of the root-hair and the soil-water in which soluble salts from the soil are dissolved. The mineral solution is weaker than the cell-sap; if this were not the case, root-absorption by osmosis could not take place. The solutions are separated from one another by the cell wall (p. 114), within which is a delicate protoplasmic lining which is *semi-permeable*—that is, it allows water to pass freely through it, but is not permeable to all the substances dissolved in the water.

The action of osmosis is difficult to understand. In the root-hair it is a vital process, regulated by the living membrane of protoplasm.

Because of this control by the protoplasmic membrane,

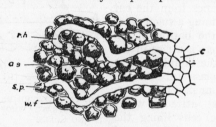

FIG. 16.—ROOT-HAIRS IN THE SOIL.

a.s., air-space; *c.*, cell of root; *r.h.*, root-hair; *s.p.*, soil particle; *w.f.*, water film.

root-hairs exercise a certain selective power in their work, with the result that some plants do not take in certain solutions that are freely absorbed by others. It is because of this selective power of roots that *rotation of crops* is the rule in agriculture. Hundreds of years before there was any science of botany, tillers of the soil avoided growing the same crop on the same land in successive years.

It is, then, as a result of osmosis, controlled by living protoplasm, that plants obtain from the *soil* one class of raw materials for the manufacture of food. From the *air* leaves take in carbon dioxide, which is necessary for the manufacture of carbohydrates within the leaf. The essential conditions for this work are the presence of sunlight and of the green colouring matter, or *chlorophyll*, in the leaves. Certain chemical reactions take place within the leaves which result in oxygen (O_2), set free from the absorbed carbon dioxide (CO_2), being returned to the air, while the carbon (C) is kept in the leaf and unites with the elements of water (H_2O) to form sugar ($C_6H_{12}O_6$) and ultimately starch ($C_6H_{10}O_5$). That oxygen is evolved during this process can be proved by collecting and testing the bubbles of gas that are given off by a water plant, such as Canadian pondweed, when it is put in a good light. Fig. 17 shows a simple arrangement for trapping the gas. The pondweed is contained in a funnel, immersed in water in a glass vessel. A test-tube full of water is inverted over the stem of the funnel. Oxygen given off from the green leaves rises in the stem of the funnel, and displaces the water. When sufficient gas has been collected it can be tested by putting the glow-

Fig. 17.—Experiment to Show the Evolution of Oxygen in Carbon-assimilation.

ing end of a splint into the test-tube. The splint then bursts into flame, thus proving that the collected gas is oxygen.

A simple experiment proves the presence of starch in green leaves; those of the lime always give good results. Two or three leaves must be picked on a sunny afternoon and kept in methylated spirits for a day or two. The green colouring matter dissolves in the alcohol, and the leaves become white. If they are dipped in iodine they turn dark blue or brownish-black. This is a proof that starch is present, for it is only on starch that iodine has this effect.

To prove that light is necessary for the manufacture of starch, two or three leaves on the tree can have black paper pinned over them, so that both sides are covered. After a few days, if they are decolorized and tested with iodine, there will be no starch reaction except at the pin-holes where a little light has penetrated.

It is equally simple to prove that chlorophyll is essential, because on testing it is found that no starch is present in a white leaf of Ivy or Geranium and that it only occurs in the green patches of the variegated leaves of Japanese Maple.

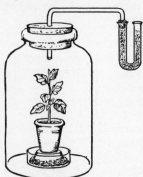

FIG. 18.—EXPERIMENT TO DEMONSTRATE THE NEED FOR CARBON DIOXIDE IN STARCH FORMATION.

Even in strong sunlight starch is not formed in green leaves if carbon dioxide is not present. This is proved by keeping a potted plant (a fuchsia, for example) in the dark for a few days, so that its leaves are free from starch. It is then placed under a large bell-jar which contains a dish of caustic potash. As is shown in Fig. 18, a tube that passes through the cork of the bell-jar is connected to a U-tube which contains soda-lime. All air that enters the bell-jar thus passes through the soda-lime, which absorbs the carbon dioxide; the carbon dioxide already within the bell-jar is absorbed by the caustic potash, thus no carbon dioxide reaches the leaves of the plant. Under these conditions no starch is formed in the leaves even when the bell-jar is in full sunlight.

This particular manufacturing process of the green plant is sometimes called *photosynthesis*, because it depends on light (Greek, *photos*, light), and sometimes *carbon assimilation*, because carbon is the foundation of the manufactured substances.

In carbon assimilation, as in respiration, there is an interchange of oxygen and carbon dioxide ; but the two processes are quite independent and must not be confused.

Respiration is an unceasing process which goes on every moment of the day and night. In it *oxygen is taken in and carbon dioxide is given out*. It is a *destructive* process of slow combustion in which energy is set free.

Carbon assimilation is a *constructive* process, in which the building up of food provides stores of potential energy (p. 37). Unlike respiration it is intermittent, for it takes place only in the light. In this process *carbon dioxide is taken in and oxygen is given out*; in the day-time, therefore, green plants are lessening the carbon dioxide content of the air and increasing its oxygen content, because in the feeding process there is a greater exchange of gases than in respiration. As daylight fades carbon assimilation ceases and only respiration is active ; the plants are then taking oxygen *from* and returning carbon dioxide *to* the outside world. It is for this reason that, in hospital wards, cut flowers and plants are removed before night falls.

In order that water in a kettle may boil, *heat* must be applied to it, and this is the *force*, or *energy*, that raises the temperature of the water to boiling point. The force upon which photosynthesis depends is *light*. When the ordinary white light of the sun passes through a glass paper-weight or a prism, it is split up into its several components—red, orange, yellow, green, blue, indigo, violet. A similar separation takes place, and a rainbow results, when the sun's rays pass through moisture suspended in the air.

Chlorophyll also causes the rays of light to separate, but whereas all the rays pass through a glass prism, some of them, the red rays in particular, are trapped and retained when light passes through chlorophyll. The radiant energy of such trapped sunlight is the force responsible for the building up of starch in green leaves, from the simple inorganic compounds of carbon dioxide and water. To-day, in the burning of coal, the sunlight thus trapped millions of years ago is set free. The light-absorbing property of chlorophyll explains why the continuation of all life on our planet is dependent upon the green plant.

It is obvious that an unlimited supply of starch cannot remain in the leaves; it is reconverted into sugar and is transported to various parts of the plant. That which is not immediately needed is stored for future use—as in seeds, for instance, in readiness for their germination (p. 107); in the potato, in readiness for its sprouting; near the bases of resting-buds, that they may have a ready supply of food when they open in the spring of the following year. As a rule when sugar reaches the various storage organs it is reconverted into starch, which is insoluble. Sometimes, however, the reserve, or some part of it, is actually stored as sugar, as in the case of the Garden Pea, Beetroot, and the Sugar-cane.

The formation of *carbohydrates* is the basic process in the green plant's manufacture of foods. *Fats* are not produced as a direct result of photosynthesis, but are formed from carbohydrates; they contain the same elements as the latter, but in different proportions. *Proteins* contain nitrogen and sulphur in addition to carbon, hydrogen, and oxygen; sometimes they contain phosphorus and other elements. All these additional elements are obtained from the soluble salts which the roots of a plant absorb with the soil-water. The energy needed for the building up of proteins is not obtained directly from the sun, as in photosynthesis, but from the breaking down of substances, chiefly carbohydrates, already formed.

As plants absorb their food-forming materials in a

liquid or gaseous state, an elaborate digestive system like that of most animals is not required. Further, as a plant does not take in a great deal more than it uses, there is little waste, except in the case of water which it given off in *transpiration* (p. 78). Other waste is got rid of in herbaceous plants when all the parts of the plant that are above ground die down at the end of its season. Most British shrubs and trees shed their leaves in autumn ; those substances that are the by-products of the plant's metabolism, and that are no longer needed, are disposed of by being passed into the leaves before they fall.

CHAPTER IX

DISTRIBUTION OF FOOD, WATER, AND AIR.
MECHANICAL SUPPORT

It has been stated that mineral solutions travel from one extreme of the plant to the other, and that manufactured foods are transported both for immediate use and for storage. It is obvious, therefore, that there must be definite and separate channels for the conduct of the mineral solutions on the one hand, and for the solutions of food on the other.

When weak mineral solutions have been absorbed from the soil by the root-hairs they travel inwards, by osmotic attraction (p. 70), passing from one living cell to another until they reach the wood, or *xylem*, through which water is carried to all parts of the plant.

Solutions of the various minerals in the soil are very weak. In order, therefore, that the necessary amount of salts may be obtained, much more water than the plant needs is absorbed, and this surplus water is got rid of by *transpiration*.

In transpiration, water, in the form of water-vapour, escapes through microscopic openings, or *stomata* (Greek, *stoma*, a mouth), which occur chiefly on the under-surfaces of leaves (Fig. 19). It is through these openings, too, that interchange of gases takes place in respiration and carbon assimilation.

Stomata are open only in the light, and this explains why many herbaceous plants—Delphiniums, for instance —often droop at the close of a hot day, but are erect the following morning: at night, through the closed stomata, no water could escape; in the dark no carbon-assimilation was taking place; therefore all the water that the roots absorbed was available for renewing turgidity.

In the day-time the activity of transpiration is remarkable. It has been estimated that from a Birch tree with approximately 200,000 leaves, 15 gallons of water are given off on an ordinary day, and as much as 85 gallons when the air is very hot and dry. One Sunflower leaf may have as many as 13,000,000 stomata, and a pint and a half of water may be lost by the plant in 12 hours.

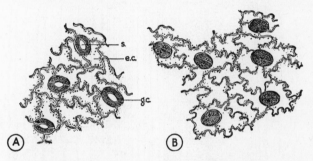

FIG. 19.—EPIDERMIS FROM THE UNDER-SURFACE OF A LEAF.
A, Leaf picked in daylight (stomata open); B, Leaf picked after being kept in the dark (stomata closed). *e.c.*, epidermal cell; *g.c.*, guard cell; *s.*, stoma.

Because of their rapid transpiration, Sunflowers have been grown in swampy soil to " drain " it.

Under the microscope wood is seen to be a tissue largely made up of tubes of extremely small diameter, whose continuity is interrupted by cross-walls. These tubes are the waterways of the plant, and result from once-living cells (p. 113) that have lost their protoplasmic contents and whose walls have undergone a chemical change, having become woody, or *lignified* (Fig. 20). Through the tubes, which may be either *tracheides* or *vessels*, water can pass freely. A tracheide is a single cell; a vessel is formed from a longitudinal row of similar cells that have formed a tube because of the degeneration of their transverse walls. The length of vessels varies greatly; in some of our forest trees (Oak) and in the lianes of tropical forests, they may be several yards long. More frequently they are at most only a few inches in length.

The path of water through the wood can be demon-

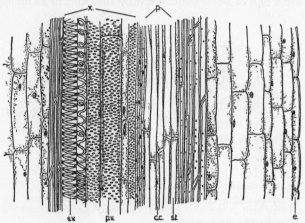

FIG. 20.—LONGITUDINAL SECTION OF STEM OF CREEPING BUTTERCUP.

c.c., companion cell; *e.*, epidermis; *p.*, phloem; *p.v.*, pitted vessel; *s.t.*, sieve tube; *s.v.*, spiral vessel; *x.*, xylem.

strated by putting the cut end of a stem into a coloured solution, such as red ink. If the stem is cut across after it has had time to take up the liquid, it is seen that the coloration is restricted to one area—this is the wood (Fig. 21).

The force that is necessary to lift water in a plant must be very great. Against the force of gravity, which is always tending to pull it back, water must be lifted even to the highest branches of the tallest trees. Many theories have been put forward in an attempt to explain the cause of this ascent; it is improbable that there is any one solution to the problem: it seems that several forces working together, no one of which would be sufficient by itself, contribute to the final result.

Weak solutions are first absorbed by the root-hairs in osmosis (p. 70). Water thus absorbed weakens the sap of the root-hairs and, as a result, water is withdrawn from them to the neighbouring cells whose sap is stronger. Thus a chain of movement through the living cells of the root is started. In this way water reaches the wood; the entry into the plant is thus a vital process dependent on living cells. Through the wood the water then travels to all parts of the plant; this passage cannot be due to osmosis because, as the vessels of the wood are dead, they are devoid of contents that could exert attraction. In plants of no great height the pressure, exerted by the roots in absorption, may be enough to drive water along its short journey to all parts, especially in spring when root-absorption is very active; but at some times of the year *root pressure* is very slight or may even be negative.

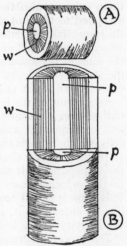

FIG. 21.—A, DIAGRAM OF A PIECE OF WOODY STEM THAT HAS STOOD IN RED INK. B, A SIMILAR STEM CUT THROUGH THE MIDDLE IN THE UPPER PART.

p., the pith which is unstained; *w.*, the wood which is stained red.

A greater force during much of the year is due to the tremendous " pull " caused by *transpiration* from the leaves. It may be difficult to realise how water can be pulled. An explanation is afforded by the " cohesion theory " : the molecules of every substance exert for each other a mutual attraction which tends to make them cohere; also the molecules of one substance are attracted to those of another substance, and this causes the respective molecules to adhere. Thus water molecules *cohere* forming columns, and the molecules adjacent to the walls of the wood *adhere* to these walls. In this way the *shape* of the water is kept intact and forms a continuous column which only a very strong force could break.

As a result of the loss of water from the surface-cells of the leaves, the osmotic pressure in their sap is increased and, consequently, water is drawn from the neighbouring cells, which, in their turn, draw it from the cells adjacent to them, so that a chain of movement is set up between the transpiring cells and the wood—a movement similar to that which follows the entry of water into the root. It is thus apparent that the exit of water from a plant, like its entry into it, is a vital process dependent upon the activity of the living cell.

The process of transpiration cannot be regarded as a disadvantage against which a plant must protect itself by all sorts of devices. The value of the transpiration current is very great : it prevents leaves from getting overheated, but, more important still, it provides for a much more rapid supply of salts to the plants than would be possible by slow diffusion.

The food that is made in the leaves of plants travels in solution through the special conducting tissue of the *phloem*, or " bast " (Fig. 22). This lies outside the wood, towards the periphery of stems and roots. Because the conducting elements have perforated cross-walls they are called *sieve-tubes*.

In plants, as in animals, food is incorporated in the protoplasm; it repairs waste; and it provides material on which all growth depends.

A constant supply of oxygen is necessary for plants as well as for animals, in order to give energy needed for growth. Substances formed in the assimilation processes must be broken down in order that the potential energy stored in them may be liberated (p. 37). The destroying agent is oxygen, on which respiration depends. Some of the liberated energy is dissipated as heat, but the greater part is used in the further growth and activities of the plant.

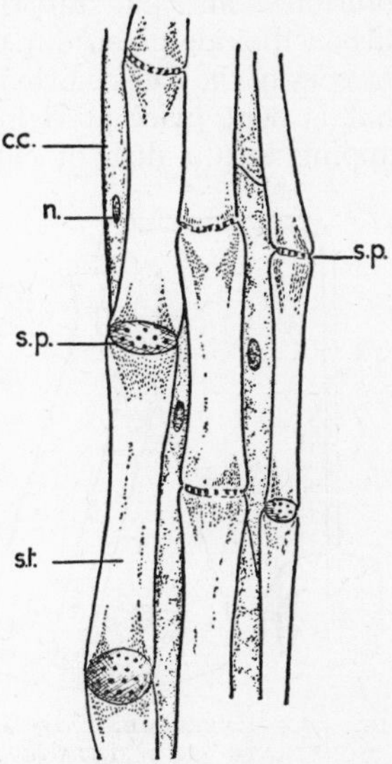

In the respiration of plants, as in the corresponding process in animals (pp. 36 *et seq.*), oxygen is taken in and carbon dioxide is given out.

To prove that carbon dioxide is *given off* in respiration a potted plant, and a beaker containing lime-water, are put under a bell-jar covered with black paper. After a time the lime-water becomes milky as a result of carbon dioxide being given off from the leaves of the plant.

FIG. 22.—LONGITUDINAL SECTION THROUGH THE PHLOEM OF THE STEM OF THE VEGETABLE MARROW.

c.c., companion cell; *n.*, nucleus; *s.p.*, sieve plate; *s.t.*, sieve tube.

Light must be excluded in this experiment in order to prevent the plant taking back, as food-making material, the carbon dioxide that is evolved (p. 74). In a control experiment, in which the plant is omitted, the lime-water remains clear.

The *intake* of oxygen in the respiratory process is

simply proved by using peas that have been soaked for a short time, and have therefore begun to germinate. Damp blotting-paper covers the bottom of a glass flask, and on this the peas are spread; a test-tube of potash solution is also put into the flask, and this absorbs the carbon dioxide given out during the process. Through the cork of the flask is fitted a piece of narrow glass tubing that is bent twice at right angles and has its free end dipping into a dish of coloured liquid (Fig. 23). The

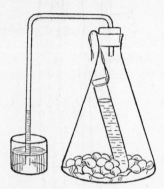

coloured solution rises slowly in the tube; this shows that the volume of air in the flask is decreasing.

The apparatus must of course be air-tight. After some days, if a lighted taper is put into the flask, it is immediately extinguished. This proves that the diminution in the volume of air in the flask is due to the loss of oxygen.

Fig. 23.—Experiment to Demonstrate the Intake of Oxygen.

In the simplest animals (*e.g.*, Amœba, Hydra) there is no need for blood and a circulatory system to carry food and oxygen. The animals are so small that simple diffusion throughout the body supplies them with all that is needed, and carries away the waste that results from respiration and feeding. In the simplest plants diffusion plays the same rôle.

The circulatory system of the higher animals may be said to have a partial counterpart in the higher plants, in the special conducting channels of the wood that carry raw materials, and in those of the bast that transport manufactured food. Even in the most highly developed plants there is no special system for the distribution of oxygen and the elimination of carbon dioxide. In many plants, as in the simplest animals, the interchange of gases takes place over the whole surface of the body. In the more highly developed forms it occurs more particularly in certain definite parts : in leaves it takes place chiefly through the stomata; in the bark of trees through special openings called *lenticels*; in roots more especially in the region of the root-hairs.

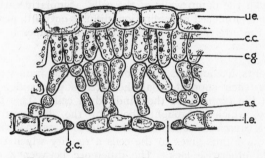

FIG. 24.—TRANSVERSE SECTION OF A LEAF.

a.s., air space; *c.c.*, columnar cell; *c.g.*, chlorophyll granule; *g.c.*, guard cell; *l.e.*, lower epidermis; *s.*, stoma; *u.e.*, upper epidermis.

In the living tissues of plants the cell-walls are always moist. In all but the youngest tissues there are gaps among the cells, known as *intercellular spaces*, which contain air and moisture. Although there is no regularity in the arrangement of intercellular spaces, they are continuous throughout a plant, providing air-ways whereby air travels to every part. Both stomata and lenticels are in direct communication with intercellular spaces (Fig. 24). For protection, the outermost walls of the covering tissue of leaves undergo a chemical change into a substance, termed *cutin*, which resembles cork. Cell-walls, however, which abut on intercellular spaces generally remain unthickened. There is little diffusion of oxygen through walls that are cuticularised, therefore, except in young plants, the gas enters by way of the stomata or the lenticels, which may therefore be regarded as organs of breathing.

Just as the cells of the animal-body are bathed in lymph which carries oxygen to them, so are the cells of plant-tissues in contact with moisture. Oxygen that has penetrated to the intercellular spaces diffuses through the damp walls of the cells. Similarly carbon dioxide, produced in respiration, diffuses outward, passes into the intercellular spaces, and finally escapes to the outside air.

Plants, like animals, need some supporting framework. For such support small herbaceous plants depend upon the *turgidity* of their individual cells. This turgidity, which is brought about by the absorption of water, causes the contents of the cells to press upon their walls and thus gives to the cells a rigidity which they would otherwise lack. The difference between a cell in a turgid and in a limp condition may be compared to the difference between a rubber hot-water bottle when it is full and when it is empty; in the former condition it acquires a certain firmness by virtue of its contents.

Turgidity is only possible in living cells which are actively carrying on osmosis (p. 70). Much of the tissue of higher plants cannot give the support of turgidity, because the cells have lost their protoplasmic contents. The supporting frame is then chiefly the tissue of the wood, which has thus a two-fold function, for as well as conducting water (p. 79) it acts as an internal skeleton.

When the trunk of a tree is cut across it is seen to be composed of wood, except for the bark on the outside and a narrow ring of softer tissue within this. As the trunk increases in girth the oldest part of the wood—

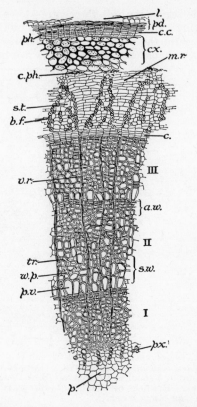

FIG. 25.—TRANSVERSE SECTION OF LIME STEM THREE YEARS
OLD. I, II, III, 1st, 2nd, AND 3rd YEARS' RINGS OF
WOOD.

a.w., autumn wood; *b.f.*, bast fibre; *c.*, cambium; *c.c.*, cork
cambium; *c.ph.*, crushed primary phloem; *cx.*, primary
cortex (collenchyma); *l.*, lenticel; *m.r.*, medullary ray; *pd.*,
cork; *ph.*, cortex; *p.v.*, pitted vessel; *px.*, primary
xylem; *s.t.*, sieve tube of secondary phloem; *s.w.*, spring wood; *tr.*,
tracheide; *v.r.*, secondary (vascular medullary) ray; *w.p.*,
wood parenchyma.

that is, the region towards the centre—loses the power of conducting water, which is carried only by the younger elements nearer the periphery. But the whole mass of the wood, both old and young, forms a solid pillar of

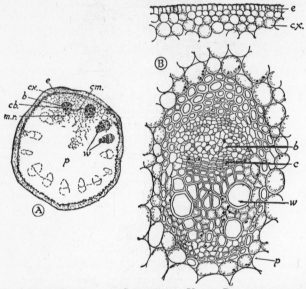

Fig. 26.—A. Transverse Section of a Young Dicotyledonous Stem (*Aristolochia*), as Seen with a Hand Lens, Showing the Ring of Vascular Bundles. B. A Drawing of one Vascular Bundle of Creeping Buttercup as seen under the Microscope.

b., bast; *cb.* or *c.*, cambium in the bundle; *cm.*, cambium forming between the bundles; *cx.*, cortex; *e.*, epidermis; *m.r.*, medullary ray; *p.*, pith; *w.*, wood.

strength that enables the tree to withstand the buffeting of wind and rain (Fig. 25).

In herbaceous plants there is not, proportionally, nearly so much wood. The transverse section of the stem of such a plant shows the wood disposed either in a ring near the edge, or in a number of separate "bundles" in a similar position. The wood is, therefore, either an unbroken cylinder, or a ring of separate strands, near the periphery of the stem (Fig. 26).

This arrangement of supporting, or "mechanical", tissue is efficient and economical. A herbaceous stem of wide diameter, which has the supporting tissue near the outside, has great mechanical advantage over a thin stem which has the same amount of supporting tissue arranged compactly; the reason is that in the former arrangement a greater surface is presented to withstand the forces of wind and rain that batter against it. It is such a plan as this that is followed in the construction of the supporting pillars of bridges. These are hollow, but have a wide circumference, so that the maximum strength results from the use of the minimum of material.

The disposition of the mechanical tissue in roots differs from that of the stem. In the case of the root there is no pressing force against which a large area of resistance is required. Instead the root is subjected to a pulling strain which tends to tear it from the earth. What is needed, therefore, is a strong resistant core, and to this end the wood is produced at the centre of a root from the first, instead of at the circumference as in stems.

CHAPTER X

RESPONSE TO OUTSIDE INFLUENCES

It is not only the so-called "sensitive plant" that responds to stimulus from without; every plant, like every animal, reacts to impressions received from the world around it.

In all but the very lowest animals reception of impressions, and their subsequent response, depends upon nerve-tissue. Even in *Hydra* (p. 125) it is claimed that there are certain "nerve cells" concerned with reception and transmission of "messages". But in even the most highly developed plants there is no tissue whose special work it is to receive impressions and control response, nor is there any central system acting as an "exchange". Plant "behaviour" depends upon some simple transmission between the contents of cells that are in contact.

In the sensitive plant there is immediate response, on the part of all the leaves of a shoot, to touch, or heat, or anæsthetics. As a result all the leaflets droop. Each leaf is made up of a number of these leaflets, arranged feather-wise on either side of a midrib. The stimulus is transmitted along the midrib of each leaflet to a cushion-like swelling at its base. As a result certain cells of the "cushion" lose water, which passes into intercellular spaces. This loss of water means loss of turgidity, and it is this that causes the leaflets to droop. The normal position is resumed when the cells of the cushion have re-absorbed water from the intercellular spaces.

This is an exceptional case showing obvious and immediate movement. In the every-day life of all plants, however, there is a restricted response of their various parts to gravity, light, water, and contact. As in the animal world the response is designed to serve some useful end.

A ready way of showing the directional response of a root and shoot to *gravity* is to dig up a Broad Bean seedling when its shoot is about 2 inches above the ground. The root must then be passed through the smallest possible hole in the cork of a gas-jar that is full of water. When the plant has grown in this normal position for about a week all connections must be made water-tight by smearing thoroughly with melted candle-grease. The jar is then supported in an upside-down position. The elongating region of roots is a little distance behind the tip, and in this region the root of the bean bends and grows downwards, obeying the gravitational force. In response to gravity most shoots grow away from the centre of the earth, and, in the experiment, the stem makes a definite bend in the

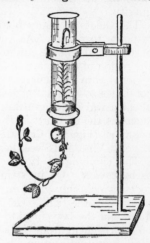

FIG. 27.—PLANT TURNED UP-SIDE DOWN TO SHOW THE CHANGE IN DIRECTION OF THE GROWTH OF ROOT AND SHOOT.

growing region and grows vertically upwards (Fig. 27). In response to the influence of gravity the lateral branches of both roots and shoots tend to assume an oblique position.

The response of roots to the stimulus of *water* is seen when mustard seeds are sprinkled in two gravy strainers, in which there is a damp layer of sawdust or coco-nut fibre. Each strainer, which must be kept damp, rests on a glass of water. In 4 or 5 days the roots are pushing through the holes and growing vertically downwards. When one strainer is removed and put over an empty glass, the roots turn upwards to the wet sawdust, and re-enter the holes of the sieve. This shows that, in this case, the attraction of water is stronger than that of gravity.

The shoots of many plants " climb " because of the response to *contact*. As a result of contact the growth of stems and tendrils is more active on the part away from the region of contact and, as a result of this more rapid regional growth, a curve results. This disparity in rate continues so long as there is growth in length, bringing about a wave of curvature, and the stem of the tendril encircles the support, as is seen in the Bindweed (Convolvulus) (Fig. 28), Clematis, Hop, Runner Bean, Black Bryony, Vine, and Sweet Pea (Fig. 29).

The climbing of Ivy is influenced by *light* as well as by *contact*. On its stem there are numbers of little roots, which only grow on the side of the stem that is away from the light. On contact they secrete a sticky fluid, and the Ivy clings to its support. The roots take no nourishment from the support; an Ivy-covered tree dies from suffocation, because the breathing holes (lenticels) of trunk and branches are covered by the climbing plant and air cannot enter.

Contact response also explains the climbing of Ampelopsis (Virginian Creeper). Here branching shoots end in flat discs which, in contact with the rough surface of a wall, produce a sticky secretion and adhere.

An entertaining experiment shows the influence of *light* on the directional growth of stems. A Broad Bean seedling is planted in a small pot placed in a saucer of water, and is put into a box that stands on end, and is covered with black paper. The lid is replaced by a sheet of black paper fixed with drawing-pins. A hole, half an inch square, is cut in this paper near the top. The box

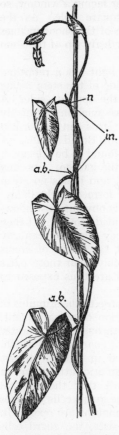

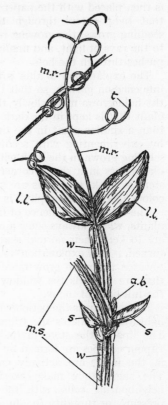

FIG. 29.—SWEET PEA CLIMBING BY TENDRILS.

a.b., axillary bud; *l.l.*, leaf-like leaflet; *m.r.*, mid-rib of the compound leaf; *t.*, tendril which is, in this case, a modified leaflet; *w.*, expansion of the stem which carries on photosynthesis.

FIG. 28.—CONVOLVULUS, SHOWING THE TWINING MAIN STEM.

a.b., axillary bud; *in.*, internode; *n.*, node.

is then placed with the paper cover facing a window, so that light enters through the square hole. As the seedling grows, the growing region of the shoot inclines to the rays of light, and finally the leafy tip of the stem pushes through the hole.

The explanation of this is that light has a retarding influence on growth, so that the side of the stem facing the hole grows more slowly than the opposite side. A plant that is kept in the dark grows much more quickly than a similar plant in the light. This can be verified by experimenting with seedlings of Broad Beans. A seedling grown in the dark will be found to be " leggy ", like plants in a shady corner of the garden. Its long stem is weak, its leaves are small, and it has no green colour, because chlorophyll is only formed in the light.

The retarding influence of light is obvious in window-plants, which always show a one-sided growth. If they are to keep their normal shape they must be regularly turned. The explanation is that the parts of stems towards the room grow more quickly than those parts that are towards the window and are thus exposed to the full light of the day.

Indirectly it is the periodic response to the stimulus of light that regulates the transpiration of a leafy plant. The lips of the stomata (p. 79) through which water vapour escapes are formed by two " guard cells " which, in the light, are actively engaged in photosynthesis. The sugar they make exerts osmotic attraction on neighbouring cells, with the result that the internal pressure, or turgidity (p. 86), of the guard cells becomes very great. Because of this, the mouths are open. In the dark, when photosynthesis ceases, the guard cells lose their turgidity and become flaccid and, as a result, the stomata are closed.

" Sleep movements ", which are characteristic of some flowers,—Wood Sorrel and Crocus, for instance— are controlled by the alternation of day and night.

The growth of sepals and petals is basal. When the flower is open the more intense light falls upon the upper—that is, the inner—surfaces of these floral leaves and, consequently, growth is here retarded. The under-surfaces, which are in comparative shade, grow more quickly than the upper surfaces, with the result that the floral leaves change their position and the flower closes. In the morning, light falls on the outer (under) surface of the leaves of the closed flower; growth is therefore more active on the inner (upper) surfaces and the flower opens.

It is obvious, however, that light cannot be the sole determining cause of such sleep movements. If it were, one would expect all flowers to close early in the day, but in most flowers that exhibit sleep-movements the closing does not take place until evening. Moreover it would be reasonable to expect that all such flowers would close at approximately the same time, and this is by no means the case—the flowers of the hedge plant, Jack-go-to-bed-at-noon, as its name implies, close in the early afternoon.

It is probable that *hormones* (p. 64), which play so important a part in animal behaviour, also control the growth of plants and are the factors which determine their various responses to outside influences. The exact nature of the stimulus that determines growth is not established, but a definite chemical substance seems to be concerned in all growth relations. This substance has been termed a *growth hormone*. An interesting experiment of Haberlandt's confirms this view. Haberlandt cut a potato and washed the surface of the wound with water, thus removing the contents of the wounded cells. Normally when a tissue has been injured cells surrounding the wound divide actively and form a protective covering layer. In this case of the cut, and *washed*, potato, no such activity occurred. Haberlandt then smeared the wound with a layer of macerated tuber, and after this treatment cell-division took place and protective tissue was formed. He concluded, therefore, that the cut cells must contain, or produce, some substance which passes into the surrounding cells and induces cell-division. He described the substance as a growth hormone, and concluded that these hormones travelled through the phloem (p. 82), because pieces of potato without phloem did not form cork over a wound.

Since Haberlandt's experiment many others have been carried out, especially on grass seedlings, all of which confirm the theory that a definite chemical substance, a " growth hormone ", is produced in parts of plants where cell-division (p. 120) is taking place and is passed along to the regions of growth. The substance may even be extracted from the plant without losing its efficiency. It does not appear to be different for every species, for in experimental work on grasses it has been proved that the substance obtained from one species may produce growth in another. It may well be that the time and rate of the closing of sepals and petals in response to variations of light, for instance, are controlled by the numbers and varieties of hormones in the basal growing regions of the sepals and petals of each particular flower.

CHAPTER XI

REPRODUCTION

THE science of Biology, more particularly perhaps on the Botanical side, has developed more slowly than Physics or Chemistry. In great measure this " lagging behind " was unavoidable, because minute investigation was impossible with the naked eye, and the progress of the science could, therefore, only follow the progress of the perfecting of lenses.

Because of this handicap the method of reproduction in plants was, for the early Botanists, a subject of conjecture merely.

Even in times long past some special virtue was assigned to the *pollen* of flowers. Some Date Palms bear only female flowers, which in due season are followed by fruits; others bear male flowers only, and these, of course, have no fruit. In ancient Greece it was the custom to assemble around fruit trees in the spring of the year and to invoke the gods, waving the while Date branches bearing male flowers. The pollen thus wafted over the female tree was looked upon as incense pleasing to the gods, whose response and approbation were later manifested in the fruitfulness of the trees. In all probability such trees would actually bear more fruit than others that were not thus visited, because pollen, the male element in fertilization, was deliberately showered over the female flowers, so that they did not depend upon the more chancy agency of wind to ensure pollination and the ultimate production of seeds.

Many centuries later Goethe, writing about pollen, came to the conclusion that its liberation was the means whereby plants got rid of their ill-humours !

The actual significance of pollen was determined accidentally when, with the aid of a hand-lens, the hairs on the central parts of the flower of the Iris were examined and slender threads were seen growing downwards from pollen that had fallen on to this part of the flower.

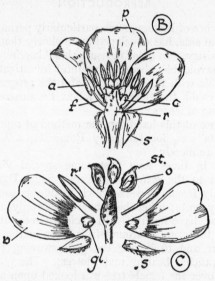

FIG. 30.—B, LONGITUDINAL SECTION OF FLOWER OF BULBOUS BUTTERCUP. C, DISSECTION OF FLOWER.

a., anther; *c.*, one carpel; *f.*, filament; *gl.*, nectary at the base of the petal; *o.*, ovary; *p.*, petal; *r.*, receptacle in section; *r'.*, whole receptacle showing scars of the removed floral leaves; *s.*, sepal; *st.*, stigma.

Pollen " dust " is not an amorphous powder but, as is seen under the microscope, is made up of thousands of definite " grains ".

The variety of floral structure is very great, and cannot be exhaustively dealt with here. Essentially every flower consists of a collection of very specially modified leaves which are borne in whorls at the tips of branches. In some cases the floral leaves are so much modified that they bear no resemblance at all to foliage leaves, although they originate in the same way. The modifications are associated with the special work of each kind of floral leaf.

The lowest or outside set of floral leaves are the *sepals*, which form the *calyx*; their function is generally protective; they enclose the rest of the flower while it is in bud and are usually simple in structure and green in colour, and in these ways resemble the foliage leaves.

Above and within the sepals are the *petals* which form the *corolla*. They are often brightly coloured and serve to attract insects which visit the flower in search of nectar.

The next set of leaves are the *stamens*, and above these are the *carpels*, which are in the centre of the flower and are at the tip of the stem. The stamens are almost always free from one another and consist of two parts, an *anther* in which *pollen* is produced and a *filament* which may be long so that it lifts the anther well above the rest of the flower. In some flowers the carpels also are free from one another (Fig. 30); in others they are partly or completely joined. Each carpel consists of a basal part, the *ovary*, in which ovules are produced; a *stigma* at the free end which

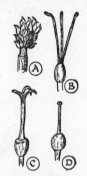

FIG. 31.—DIFFER-ENT FORMS OF PISTIL.

A, The pistil of the buttercup: made up of many free carpels. B, The pistil of the bladder campion: made up of three joined carpels, whose styles and stigmas are free. C, The pistil of the Canterbury bell: made up of three joined carpels, whose stigmas are free. D, The pistil of the primrose: made up of five carpels completely joined.

receives pollen from the anthers, and an intermediate part, the *style*, which connects the ovary and stigma. The carpels may be free from one another, or more or less completely joined : in Pinks the ovaries only are joined, leaving the styles and stigmas free ; in a Canter-

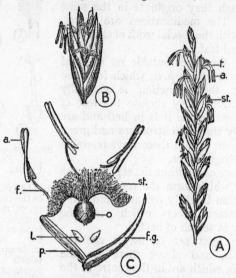

FIG. 32.—WIND-POLLINATED FLOWERS OF THE COUCH GRASS. A, WHOLE EAR. B, SPIKELET. C, ONE FLOWER DISSECTED. *a.*, anther; *f.*, filament; *f.g.*, fertile glume; *l.*, lodicule; *o.*, ovary; *p.*, pale; *st.*, stigma.

bury Bell the stigmas only are free ; in the Primrose the carpels are completely joined (Fig. 31). The whole collection of carpels make up the pistil.

The stamens and carpels are the essential parts of the flower, for without them no seeds could be produced.

The simplest flowers have neither sepals nor petals ; such flowers are characteristic of all grasses (Fig. 32), and of many trees (Fig. 37), the Hazel, for instance and the Willow (Fig. 33). Flowers which consist of all the floral parts and which have all their parts separated are illus-

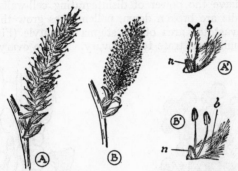

FIG. 33.—THE SALLOW WILLOW. A, FEMALE INFLORESCENCE (CATKIN). B, MALE INFLORESCENCE (CATKIN). A′, FEMALE FLOWER. B′, MALE FLOWER.

b., bract; *n.*, honey gland.

trated by the Buttercup (Fig. 30). Many flowers, however, are more complex in structure: in the Poppy, for instance, the carpels are joined; in the Foxglove (Fig. 38) and Primrose (Fig. 34) the petals also are joined, and to this joined corolla the stamens are attached.

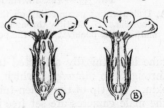

As in the sexual reproduction of animals, the act of fertilization is the fusion of two gametes. The male gamete is produced in a pollen-grain, and the female is

FIG. 34.—LONGITUDINAL SECTIONS OF PRIMROSE FLOWERS. A, THRUM-EYED. B, PIN-EYED.

the egg-cell of an ovule. Pollen is deposited on the stigma and, in order that the gametes may meet, there grows from each pollen-grain a hollow thread, the *pollen-tube*, which bears two male gametes at its tip where special ferments, or *enzymes* (p. 20), are produced; these have the power of disintegrating cell-walls. As the walls are broken down, pollen-tubes grow through the devastated area of the stigma and style (Fig. 35) and finally penetrate to the ovary. In the ovary each

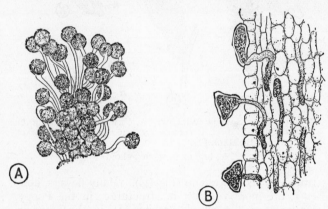

FIG. 35.—GERMINATING POLLEN GRAINS.

A, Pollen grains germinating on the tip of the stigma of Escholtzia. B, Section through stigma of Evening Primrose, showing the penetration of the pollen tubes.

tube is chemically attracted to an ovule and enters it through the *micropyle*, which is a minute hole in the skin. The tip of the pollen-tube then breaks down, and the male gametes are set free in close proximity to the egg-cell (Fig. 36), with which one of them fuses.

In-breeding is avoided by dog-fanciers and on stud-farms, because it produces weak offspring. Such in-breeding is prevented in the vast majority of Flowering Plants by certain devices that prevent the pollen of a flower from fertilizing the ovules of the same flower.

Self-fertilization is made impossible in many flowers by the stamens and ovules becoming mature at different times. In others the anthers of the stamens are at too low a level in the flower for their pollen to fall upon the stigmas. Obviously, again, self-pollination cannot take place in flowers like those of the Date, Willow and Hazel, which are unisexual.

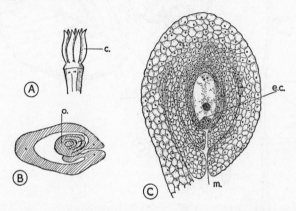

FIG. 36.—MARSH MARIGOLD. A, THE PISTIL. B, TRANSVERSE SECTION OF A SINGLE CARPEL. C, SECTION THROUGH ONE OVULE MORE HIGHLY MAGNIFIED.

c., carpel; *e.c.*, egg-cell; *m.*, micropyle; *o.*, ovule.

In many plants, as in the Date and Willow, staminate flowers and pistillate flowers are borne on separate trees. In other cases both male and female flowers grow on the same plant, as in the Hazel, whose male flowers are arranged in hanging, tassel-like " catkins " that shake in the wind. These catkins are the familiar " lambs' tails " of our hedgerows in the spring. The female flowers of the Hazel are in the centre of a leaf-bud, but their red stigmas stick out in a tuft through the tip of the bud (Fig. 37).

As self-fertilization is generally a difficulty, and is often actually an impossibility, there must be some " go-

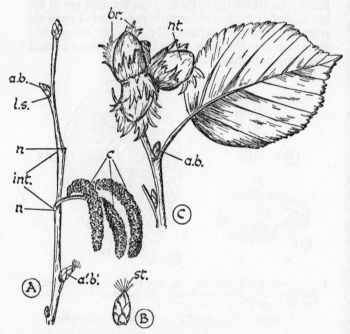

FIG. 37.—A, TWIG OF HAZEL IN EARLY SPRING. B IS *a'.b'*., ENLARGED. C, TWIG OF HAZEL IN AUTUMN, ALL OF WHICH HAS GROWN FROM B.

a.b., axillary bud in the axil of the simple leaf; *a'.b'.*, axillary bud within which are the flowers with carpels (female); *br.*, cupule round the fruit which is a nut; *c.*, catkins of flowers that have stamens (male); *int.*, internode; *l.s.*, leaf-scar; *n.*, node; *nt.*, nut; *st.*, red stigmas.

between " to carry pollen from one flower to another. In our country the carriers are either insects or the wind.

Flowers that are wind-pollinated are unisexual and dull in colour, as in the Hazel; they have no scent and produce no honey. The flowers of grasses and of most of our trees are in this category. There is so much waste of pollen when it is blown by the wind that it is produced in great quantity, often in rather loosely attached anthers of long stamens that are readily swayed by a breeze. The stigma of the female flowers protrude somewhat to catch the pollen as it is floating by, and they are often hairy so that they retain the pollen that is caught.

The flowers of the catkins of the Willow (the so-called " palm "), unlike the majority of tree-flowers, have honey-glands, or *nectaries*, and are therefore visited and pollinated by insects (Fig. 33). Poplars are close relations of the Willows and they are pollinated by wind; their catkins, like the male catkins of Birch and Hazel, are long and pendulous.

Flowers that are pollinated by insects are usually conspicuous because of their size and their colour; many of them have a sweet smell, and they provide either nectar or surplus pollen as food for their insect visitors.

So very many flowers show most interesting adaptations for cross-pollination by insects that it is difficult to decide which to select for detailed description. Perhaps the Foxglove is as good a choice as any, for it is a common plant, everybody knows it well, and its flowers are large. This flower has five joined, green sepals, and five petals, somewhat irregular in size and shape, which unite to form the fairies' " glove "—for the flower is supposed to get its name from the German *Volk*, in its meaning of the " fairy folk ".

The various markings inside the corolla guide the visiting bee to the nectar, which is at the base of the flower around the ovary. Four stamens, two long and two short, grow on the shorter upper lip of the petals (Fig. 38); their anthers are ripe and set free their pollen before the stigma is mature. The stigma is two-cleft, and the style that bears it is long and slender.

A bee enters the flower head first, pushing its way

FIG. 38.—THE INFLOR-ESCENCE OF THE FOX-GLOVE (RACEME).

g.p., the growing point. The outlined flower shows self-pollination taking place when cross-pollination has failed. As the corolla slips off, the anthers leave pollen on the stigmas which they rub against in passing.

along the lower lip of the petals; when it has taken the nectar it needs it withdraws from the flower backwards. Both on entering and leaving it brushes against the over-arching stamens, with the result that pollen from the anthers is rubbed on to its hairy back. The bee may visit several flowers in this way, collecting more and more pollen. But on a lower level of the inflorescence, or on that of another plant, it will certainly enter a flower in which the stamens have given up all their pollen and are withering. In such a flower the stigma is now mature and is in the same position as were the anthers previously. On this visit, therefore, the bee brushes against the stigma and, as this is rather sticky, pollen-grains from the insect's back are deposited on the two stigmatic lobes.

Pollination may be defined as the carrying of pollen from the anthers of a flower to the stigma, either of the same flower (*self-pollination*), or of another flower *of the same kind* (*cross-pollination*).

A pollen-grain has a two-layered coat. The inner layer is extremely thin; the outer layer, which is much firmer and thicker, has weak places here and there. From the stigma the grains absorb a sugary solution and swell, so that the outer coat bursts at one of the thin places; the inner coat then bulges through the break, just as the inner tube of the tyre of a car or bicycle may be forced through a cut in the outer cover. The "bulge" is the beginning of the pollen-tube, which carries the male gamete to the egg.

As a result of the stimulus set up by fertilization great changes take place : the ovary becomes the *fruit*; the ovule becomes the *seed*; the fertilized egg develops into the *embryo*. It frequently happens that parts surrounding the ovary are affected by the act of fertilization and become part of the fruit : in the Apple the true fruit is the core; the juicy, sweet part that is eaten is actually stem, which has grown very much and encloses the true fruit.

It does not always happen that every ovule in an ovary is fertilized. In shelling peas a small unfertilized pea is often found at one end of a pod; such a "failure" cannot, of course, give rise to a new plant because, as there has been no fusion of gametes, no embryo has been formed.

Fertilization results, not only in the production of an embryo, but also in the production of a certain amount of food for use in the early stages of germination. Before the root is provided with root-hairs for the absorption of water from the soil, and before the shoot has green leaves to carry on the work of carbon-assimilation, the young plant is dependent upon this initial food that is made available for absorption by the action of enzymes. The storage is sometimes in the embryo itself: in Peas and Beans sugar and starch are stored in the two fleshy lobes that we eat and that, although they are scarcely recognizable as such, are the first leaves of the new plant. In the nut of the Hazel proteins and oils are not in the embryo itself, but in the tissue that surrounds it; such a supply of food reaches its maximum in the white, fleshy bulk of the Coconut.

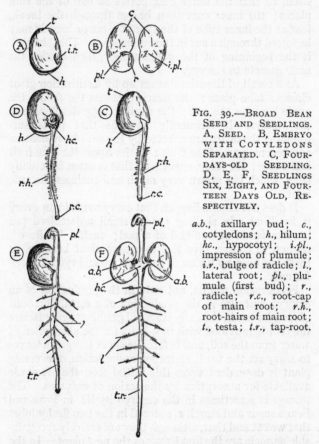

FIG. 39.—BROAD BEAN SEED AND SEEDLINGS. A, SEED. B, EMBRYO WITH COTYLEDONS SEPARATED. C, FOUR-DAYS-OLD SEEDLING. D, E, F, SEEDLINGS SIX, EIGHT, AND FOURTEEN DAYS OLD, RESPECTIVELY.

a.b., axillary bud; *c.*, cotyledons; *h.*, hilum; *hc.*, hypocotyl; *i.pl.*, impression of plumule; *i.r.*, bulge of radicle; *l.*, lateral root; *pl.*, plumule (first bud); *r.*, radicle; *r.c.*, root-cap of main root; *r.h.*, root-hairs of main root; *t.*, testa; *t.r.*, tap-root.

Because of its size a Broad Bean is useful for studying the structure of a seed. It consists of two parts : the *testa*, which is the much-thickened wall of the ovule, and the *embryo* which it encloses. When the seed has been soaked and the testa removed only the embryo remains. It consists of :—

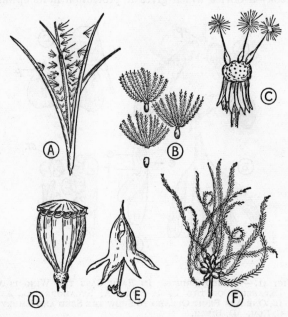

FIG. 40.—A, FRUIT OF WILLOW-HERB, SHOWING HAIRY SEEDS.
B, FRUITS OF THISTLE. C, FRUITS OF DANDELION. D, FRUIT OF POPPY. E, FRUIT OF CAMPANULA, WHOSE PORES CLOSE IN WET WEATHER. F, FRUITS OF CLEMATIS.

1. Two large fleshy lobes attached on either side of a very short axis. These are the seed leaves or *cotyledons*, the first leaves of the new plant. On treatment with iodine it is seen that they store starch.

2. The young root, or *radicle*, which points directly

downwards. From this the whole root-system of the plant develops.

3. The rudimentary bud, or *plumule*, which grows directly upwards; at first this is bent like a crochet-hook—a device which gives it protection in its upward

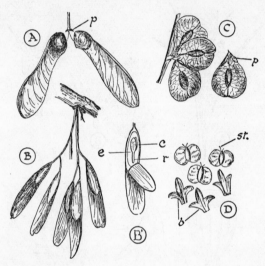

FIG. 41.—WINGED FRUITS. IN EACH CASE THE WING IS AN EXPANSION OF THE FRUIT-COAT. A, SYCAMORE. B, ASH. B', ONE ASH FRUIT OPENED TO SHOW THE SEED AND EMBRYO. C, ELM. D, BIRCH.

b., bracts; *c.*, cotyledons; *e.*, endosperm; *p.*, remains of perianth; *r.*, root; *st.*, persistent stigmas.

push through the soil. From the plumule the shoot portion of the plant—leaves, flowers and fruit—eventually develops (Fig. 39).

A young plant is thus well equipped for its initial growth, and it only remains for it to reach a suitable spot in which to stake a claim. This would be an impossibility if there were not some means of ensuring the distribution of seeds over a fairly wide area.

In such distribution the wind plays an important part. So that they may float lightly in the air, seeds of Willow, Poplar, and Willow-herb are furnished with silky hairs. The " clock " of the Dandelion is a head of fruits each containing one seed; the slender column above each fruit is crowned with a ring of hairs that acts as a parachute (Fig. 40). Many fruits, and some seeds, have " wings "

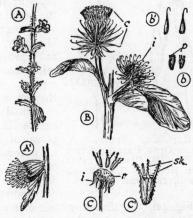

Fig. 42.—Fruits with Adhesive Appendages. A, Part of Inflorescence of Agrimony. A′, One Fruit with Strong De-curved Hairs on the Receptacle. B, Burdock. C, Receptacle and Fruits of Bur-marigold. C′, One Fruit Enlarged.

b., fruits of Burdock; b′., hooked bracts of Burdock; c., head of flowers; i., bracts; r., receptacle; sk., barbed spikes.

which make it easy for them to be blown by the wind. The winged fruits of Sycamore, Maple, Ash, and Birch are very familiar (Fig. 41). In the Scotch Pine, Gladiolus, and Bignonia it is the seeds that are winged.

In annuals there is not quite the same need as in perennials for such wide distribution, because the future seedlings will not have to compete with their ancestors. It is common, therefore, for the seeds of annuals to be scattered by simple swaying in the wind of the stalk that supports the fruit : in Poppies the seeds escape through a ring of holes at the top of the fruit; in the Wallflower they are blown by the wind, or washed by the rain, from the flat septum on which they grow.

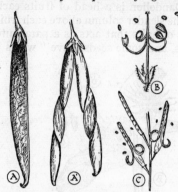

FIG. 43.—EXPLOSIVE FRUITS. A, CLOSED AND OPEN PODS OF EVER-LASTING PEA. B, OPENING FRUIT OF HERB ROBERT. C, OPENING FRUITS OF BITTERCRESS.

Animals act as agents in the dispersal of fruits that have some form of adhesive appendage, as in the " burrs " of Goosegrass and Burdock (Fig. 42). Again many cases of seed-dispersal depend, not upon an external agent, but upon some mechanism in the fruit itself : seeds are forcefully expelled from the fruits of Violet and Wood Sorrel, and some Geranium species; the rapid spread of Balsams in a garden is due to the violence with which the seeds are catapulted from the fruits; in many plants of the Pea-family the expulsion of seeds is brought about by the sudden separation and twisting of the two halves of the pod (Fig. 43); at noon on a summer day, one hears repeated pops and rustles among the Gorse bushes; the " pop " is the sudden opening of the pod; the " rustle " is the contact of the far-flung seeds with the undergrowth.

SECTION III

THE WIDE WORLD OF LIVING THINGS: THEIR STRUCTURE, RANGE, AND VARIETY

CHAPTER XII

CELLULAR STRUCTURE

THE term "tissues" is known to everyone. What is not such a familiar conception is the fact that tissues of living things are made up of very minute cells. Cells have been defined as "the units of organic structure". They may be compared to the bricks of which a building is composed, for, similarly, the cells are the units of the structure which is the living body.

The vital constituent of every cell is *protoplasm*, which, in the last century, was defined by Professor Thomas H. Huxley as "the physical basis of life". The word itself means "first form", and aptly suggests the basic nature of protoplasm. An Oak Tree, Mould on jam, a Fern, a Delphinium, a Slug, a Centipede, an Adder, a Thrush, a Rabbit, and Man himself, all started life as one microscopically minute speck of protoplasm.

The actual chemical composition of protoplasm is known. It contains, among others, the elements Carbon, Hydrogen, Oxygen, Nitrogen, Phosphorus, and Sulphur. But protoplasm is much more than a mere combination of certain chemical elements. Its essential characteristic is its "livingness", and in analysis it is, of necessity, killed. Therefore although various attempts have been made to construct protoplasm in the laboratory, all have failed, and the mystery of life is still a secret.

Those who have even a simple microscope will be

able to see living protoplasm if water containing *Amœba* (p. 123) is mounted on a slide and covered with a slip.

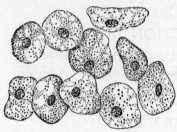

FIG. 44.—CELLS FROM THE LINING OF THE CHEEK.

The grey, formless body of an *Amœba* " flows " across the field of vision. Moving protoplasm can also be seen if a leaf of the American Pondweed is similarly mounted. A few moments must be allowed for the leaf to recover from the shock of amputation; then, in the long cells towards the middle of the leaf, the circulation of the protoplasm can be seen. These are two outstanding cases of protoplasmic movement which, generally speaking, is much too slow to be discernible.

A distinction between the cells of plants and animals is that almost all plant-cells are bounded by a wall, whereas animal-cells have no such boundary (Fig. 44). When a Privet berry ripens, the cells of the pulp separate one from another. If the pulp be mounted in water, something of the structure of

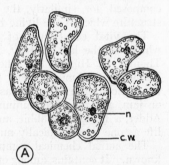

FIG. 45.—CELLS FROM THE PULP OF A PRIVET BERRY.

A, mounted in water. *c.w.*, cell wall; *n.*, nucleus.

the cells can be made out, even with a hand lens. Each cell is seen to be surrounded by a wall, which encloses granular-looking protoplasm coloured purple by the cell-sap. As in all living cells, there is a smaller, denser body, the *nucleus* (Fig. 45).

Actually the term " cell " for the units of plant and animal life is not a particularly good one. In the seventeenth century plant tissues were, for the first time, examined under magnifying lenses, and what most impressed the Botanists of the period was their superficial resemblance to the cells of a honeycomb. With their inadequate lenses they could see very little of the contents of the " spaces ", and came to the conclusion that the obvious boundaries were the important parts of the tissues. Under this misapprehension they gave the term " cell " to the cavities, and for more than 300 years it has remained in the nomenclature of Biology.

One such cell constitutes the whole body of the simplest animals and plants, as in *Amœba* and *Chlamydomonas* (pp. 123, 163). In multicellular organisms the cells are not uniform in character, and cells of a like nature occur in definite systems. Even in such a simple animal as *Hydra* there is differentiation in the outer and inner cells of its two-layered body-wall (p. 124).

In animals and plants of greater complexity there is always a definite protective tissue on the outside of the organisms; within are certain tissues concerned with transport, and others that give support to the body.

In the higher plants transport depends upon wood and bast (pp. 79, 82), and support is given by the wood and by tissues whose cells are in a condition of turgidity (p. 86). The covering tissue of leaves and of young stems is the *epidermis*, which is a single cell-layer. The outermost walls of the cells undergo a chemical change, becoming " cuticularized ", so that their protective function is increased. The cuticle is most pronounced in leaves of evergreens—Ivy, Laurel, Holly, for instance —which are thus able to withstand the rigours of winter.

On the older parts of woody perennials the epidermis would be quite inadequate as a protective tissue, and it is supplanted by " bark " on the trunks and branches of trees. Under the epidermis certain cells divide to form a layer of cork. As this is impermeable to water, all tissue outside the cork is cut off from supplies and dies. Each year a new cork-layer is formed, with the result that the dead tissue, or bark, increases in thickness. It would be fatal for the plant if the air-supply were also intercepted, and therefore there is communication with the atmosphere by means of *lenticels* (Fig. 25). The formation of cork reaches its maximum in the trunk of the Cork Oak. The most obvious lenticels are the brown transverse markings that show up so clearly on the shiny bark of the Silver Birch.

Because the higher animals lead more active lives than plants, they exhibit, as would be expected, greater tissue-differentiation. Muscle, nerve, bone, blood, fat, skin, are all tissues of the bodies of higher animals.

In carving meat it is obvious that the flesh, which is muscle, is made up of bundles of fibres. These are, in their turn, made up of thousands of cells. Muscle-cells have the power of contraction and expansion; they can become shorter and thicker, and they can elongate, thus becoming correspondingly thinner. When the cells contract there is a " pull " at the point where the muscle is attached to bone, either directly or by a non-contractile *tendon*. Such a tendon is seen in carving a shoulder of mutton; it is tough and shiny and connects the lean meat—that is, the muscle—to the ridge of the shoulder-blade (p. 46). When muscles contract, the supporting bones act as levers, moving one upon another. When the arm is bent at the elbow, the contraction and thickening of the biceps muscle can be felt as the radius, to which one end of it is attached, is drawn upwards. The muscle relaxes when the arm is unbent and the hand allowed to drop.

Muscular tissue, like all other tissues of the body, carries on its work because it is supplied with food brought to it by the blood, and because its accumulated potential energy can be converted into kinetic energy as a result of the action of oxygen; the oxygen is carried by arterial blood to all cells and the waste products of their action are then removed by the veins.

The blood which performs this essential work is itself a tissue, for, as already stated (p. 26), it consists of many thousands of cells in a fluid " matrix ".

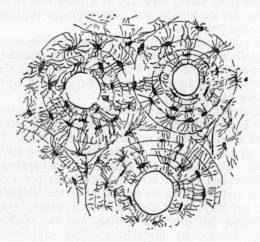

FIG. 46.—TRANSVERSE SECTION OF BONE.

Bone is also a tissue (Fig. 46). Whereas in blood the cells are disposed in a fluid, in bone they are embedded in a very hard matrix, impregnated with various inorganic salts, of which calcium phosphate is the chief. There are hundreds of living cells in the hard matrix. If it were not so, if the skeleton were composed entirely of non-living matter, there could be no growth of bone and no " knitting " of a broken limb. Of necessity the living cells must be supplied with oxygen and food.

But blood cannot permeate the matrix. For this reason the cells are arranged in concentric circles around canals, each of which contains an artery and a vein. Extremely fine channels radiate out from the central canal and carry blood to and from the living cells. The general plan is seen when a broken piece of dead bone is examined. The tubes with which it is riddled are the canals that in life contained the blood-vessels. Around these tubes, especially if a hand lens is used, minute pits are visible, and these mark the position of the former living cells.

The growth of bones may take place in three regions. In vertebræ and in the long bones of the skeleton it occurs at each end of the bone as well as in the shaft, and is regulated by hormones (p. 64) secreted by the pituitary gland (p. 62).

The skin that covers, binds, and protects the whole of the body conforms much more closely to the general idea of a tissue than do muscle, blood, and bone. It is made up of many layers of cells that form two distinct regions. The outermost of these is the dead *epidermis*; the innermost is the *dermis*, whose cells are living. Dermis and epidermis are in contact at the Malpighian layer, but they do not meet on an even plane, because the dermis has a waved outline, and the epidermis closely follows its inequalities. This explains the " prints " at the finger-tips of man, which are so characteristic that they are not alike in any two individuals.

The living cells of the Malpighian layer are continually dividing (p. 119), and as new cells are formed the older ones are pushed nearer to the surface. In time these die, losing their protoplasm and nuclei. They then form the horny, corneous layer of the skin (Lat. *cornu*, horn). The dead cells may separate from the surface as " scurf " or they may form a horny layer which, in Man, is particularly thick at the heel and behind the big toe. There are neither nerves nor blood-vessels in these dead layers; no pain is felt and there is no flow of blood when they are cut. Hairs and nails, claws, scales, and feathers are all special modifications of this horny layer of the skin.

Through the action of sweat-glands (p. 62) the skin helps to regulate body temperature and to get rid of a certain amount of waste. It has also a protective function, for there is no danger of bacterial infection through the skin unless it is punctured. It is well to apply iodine, or other antiseptic, to the slightest scratch, and so prevent bacterial attack. This is particularly wise if the skin is broken in gardening, for one species of the *Tetanus bacillus* is common in garden soil and, although it is a comparatively rare occurrence, there have been many cases of death from lockjaw resulting from neglect of this simple precaution.

Another important function of the skin is to receive impressions of touch. Just below the epidermis are the finely branched endings of nerves that communicate either with the brain or the spinal cord. In the case of the burning match (p. 52) an impression of pain is received by nerve-endings under the skin, the message passes with the utmost rapidity to the central nervous system, the appropriate sequence results, and the match is dropped.

It has already been stated that every multicellular animal and plant, no matter what may be its ultimate complexity, begins life as one single cell. All tissues of mature organisms have been formed by repeated divisions of similar cells, followed by certain chemical and physical changes, so that widely different structures, such as bone, skin, blood, wood, bast, and so on, have been produced.

Cell-division is in no way a simple splitting into two. In order that the two resulting " daughter "-cells may have all the properties of the " parent "-cell, it is essential that there should be an exact apportioning of these properties.

Such cell-divisions are initiated by the nucleus which divides in a very complicated way, while the surrounding protoplasm is merely halved.

The nucleus contains deeply-staining protoplasmic matter, to which the name *chromatin* has been given.

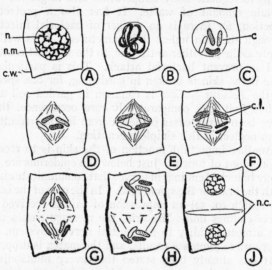

FIG. 47.—DIAGRAMS ILLUSTRATING CELL-DIVISION : FOUR CHROMOSOMES ARE REPRESENTED.

A–J, Successive stages in division. *c.*, chromosome; *c.l.*, chromosome divided longitudinally; *c.w.*, cell-wall; *n.*, nucleus; *n.c.*, new cells resulting from the division; *n.m.*, nuclear membrane.

It is the chromatin that carries, in its various regions, all individual characteristics—the colour of hair and eyes, for instance; the amiable or disagreeable temperament; the form of flowers, fruits and seeds; the complete equipment of the individual, in fact.

In a non-dividing (resting) nucleus the chromatin

looks like a net-work; when division takes place the chromatin material divides into a number of parts called *chromosomes*, whose number is constant for every species of plant or animal. There are, for instance, forty-seven chromosomes in every nucleus of a male human being, and forty-eight in the nuclei of the female. In the Frog the number of chromosomes is twenty-four; in the Apple there are thirty-four and in the Hyacinth sixteen.

In the early stages of cell-division (*mitosis*) the chromosomes arrange themselves evenly on the equator of a " spindle " that appears in each cell. Each chromosome then splits lengthwise, the halves separate from each other, and travel to opposite poles of the parent-cell (Fig. 47). Here the half-chromosomes unite, with the result that two daughter-cells, one at each pole, are formed from the original parent. There is strong evidence in support of the theory that chromosome-constituents, known in genetic language as *genes*, bear particular individual qualities, and that these genes have a linear arrangement in the chromosomes. Therefore only a *lengthwise* split of the chromosomes, into identical halves, could ensure accurate and equal distribution of the particular qualities to the two daughter-nuclei and, therefore, to all the body-cells of any organism.

When fertilization takes place the chromosomes of a male and female gamete fuse to form the nucleus of the fertilized egg. Nevertheless the number of chromosomes is not doubled in each succeeding generation; the explanation of this is that the division of the mother-cells of gametes follows a different course from that of the " body-cells ".

In the formation of gametes there is always one preceding cell-division (*meiosis*) in which the chromosomes do not split. When, for instance, a nucleus in the testis of an Earthworm divides to form male gametes, there is no longitudinal partition of the chromosomes, but one half of their number passes to each pole of the spindle to form the nucleus of each resulting gamete (Fig. 48). Each gamete, therefore, has half the body-number of

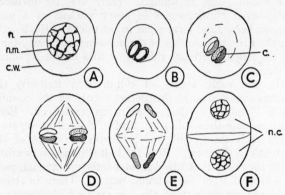

Fig. 48.—Diagrams Illustrating Cell-Division in which the Number of Chromosomes is Reduced to Half.

A–F, Successive stages in division. The original number of chromosomes is here represented as four, the reduced number is two. *c.*, chromosome; *c.w.*, cell-wall; *n.*, nucleus; *n.c.*, new cells resulting from the division; *n.m.*, nuclear membrane.

whole chromosomes, instead of the whole number of halves, as in ordinary cell-division. In this way the number of chromosomes in every species is kept constant from one generation to another.

CHAPTER XIII

NUTRITION

FUNDAMENTALLY nutrition takes place in the same way throughout the whole of the animal kingdom. No animal can build up its own food from simple, inorganic substances. Even such a simple animal as *Amœba*, like the highest animal, Man, needs ready-made carbo-

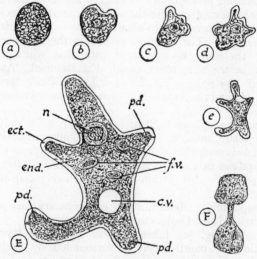

FIG. 49.—AMŒBA.

a–e, diagrams of an encysted Amœba, gently warmed by holding the slide on the warmed hand. Its successive movements were then noted and drawn. E is *e* highly magnified. *c.v.*, contractile vacuole; *ect.*, ectoplasm; *end.*, endoplasm; *f.v.*, food vacuoles with ingested particles; *n.*, nucleus; *pd.*, pseudopodia. F shows binary fission.

hydrates, proteins, and fats (Chap. I); these must be taken in by the animal and changed into simpler soluble substances that can be absorbed.

In unicellular animals feeding is a simple process. *Amœba* (Fig. 49) needs no digestive tract for its intake of food and output of waste matter. In its flowing motion it may engulf any particle of organic substance, even a smaller *Amœba*, with which it comes in contact. Two protoplasmic extensions, or *pseudopodia*, enclose the particle, together with the minutest drop of water, thus forming within the body a " food vacuole "; into this pass enzymes (p. 20) which are secreted by the surrounding protoplasm and which bring about the digestion of the captive. As the work of digestion proceeds, a change from acidity to alkalinity has been detected in the vacuole. The digestive process in the food vacuole may, therefore, be compared with that which takes place in the alimentary canal of a Mammal. At the end of the process the digested food diffuses through the body and the *Amœba* flows away from any undigested part.

Such a simple method of feeding is possible only for unicellular animals. The plan of all multicellular animals is such that there is an aperture, through which food passes to a cavity where it is digested. After this the products of digestion must reach every cell of the body.

Simple multicellular animals have one aperture only; through this food enters and waste passes out.

Hydra (Fig. 50) takes in food through a terminal opening, or mouth, that is surrounded by tentacles which help in the capture of minute water-creatures. Like its near relations, the " Jelly Fishes ", it is provided with offensive weapons that sting and paralyse the prey before it is swept into the body-cavity. In the water of the cavity the captives are partially dissolved, because some of the cells lining it secrete enzymes.

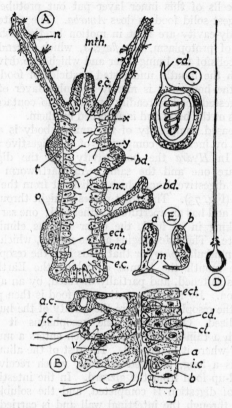

FIG. 50.—HYDRA.

A, Vertical section. B, The part *xy* much magnified. C, Stinging
apparatus. D, The stinging hair. E, The cells *a, b* of the
ectoderm with muscle-tails. *a.c.*, amœboid cell; *bd.*, Hydra
bud; *cl., cd.*, parts of the stinging apparatus; *ect.*, ectoderm;
end., endoderm; *e.c.*, cavity; *f.c.*, flagellate cell; *i.c.*, intersti-
tial cell : these cells give rise to structures of different characters; *m.*, muscle process; *mth.*, mouth; *n.*, stinging apparatus;
nc., nucleus; *o.*, ovary; *t.*, testis; *v.*, vacuole.

Other cells of this inner layer put out protuberances and ingest solid food as does *Amœba*. The contents of the body-cavity are kept in motion by the lashing of whips of protoplasm, the *flagella*, which extend from many cells of the lining-layer and which also drive out, through the mouth, undigested particles of food. Because the body-wall is merely a double layer of cells, the digested food is readily brought into contact with all cells of the body and is absorbed by them.

Increased complexity of the animal body is accompanied by increased complexity of the digestive apparatus. In *Hydra* the body-cavity and the digestive tract are one and the same. An Earthworm has a special digestive tract which is distinct from the body-cavity (Fig. 73). This tract passes straight through the animal and has an aperture at either end; one serves for the taking in of food, the other for the elimination of waste. The tract begins at the mouth, which opens into a muscular *pharynx* that leads into the œsophagus. In the mouth the humus on which the Earthworm feeds is softened, and partially digested, by an alkaline secretion. By muscular action the food is then pushed along the œsophagus, where the acidity of the humus is neutralized. On leaving the œsophagus it passes through a thin-walled *crop* and then enters a muscular *gizzard* where it is crushed. The rest of the alimentary tract is a long, uncoiled *intestine*, which receives the ground-up food from the gizzard. In the intestine the work of digestion is completed, and the soluble food passes through the intestinal wall and is carried to all parts of the body by the blood (Fig. 51).

Special modifications of the alimentary tract of Birds are essential, because they have no teeth. From the mouth the food passes down the œsophagus into a thin-walled *crop*, where it is stored and softened. When it reaches the *stomach* it is acted upon by gastric juices. From the stomach food passes to the *gizzard*, which has thick muscular walls and a horny lining; here the food is ground up with the aid of small stones which the bird has swallowed and which help to compensate for the absence of teeth. Grit of some kind must always be given to cage-birds with their food.

A Bird's digestion is almost perfect; it eats little that is unprofitable and the amount of waste matter,

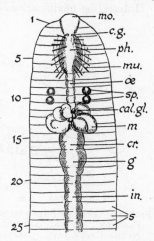

FIG. 51.—DISSECTION OF THE ANTERIOR END OF AN EARTHWORM FROM THE DORSAL SIDE.

cal.gl., glands whose secretions neutralise the acid in the humus that passes along the œsophagus; *c.g.*, the rudimentary " brain "; *cr.*, crop; *g.*, gizzard; *in.*, intestine; *m.*, part of male reproductive organs; *mo.*, mouth; *mu.*, muscles of pharynx; *œ.*, œsophagus; *ph.*, pharynx; *s.*, segments; *sp.*, spermathecae.

or *fæces*, is small. The whitish, semi-solid pellets, often called " bird-lime ", are waste expelled partly from the food canal and partly from the kidneys. It is from the accumulated excreta of successive generations of birds, which have lived in large numbers undisturbed for countless ages, that the guano deposits have been formed. These deposits are rich in nitrogenous matter and are now worked for the production of manures.

Among Mammals there are characteristic differences in the teeth and alimentary tracts of those that are carnivorous and those that are herbivorous. As the digestion of carbohydrates begins in the mouth (p. 19), herbivorous animals must have good grinding teeth; these, therefore, are broad and have ridged surfaces that are efficient for grinding. Flesh-eaters, on the other hand, have teeth with sharp fangs for tearing flesh; grinding teeth are not needed, because digestion of proteins begins in the stomach; this explains why Dogs " bolt their food ".

Interesting modifications occur in certain herbivorous

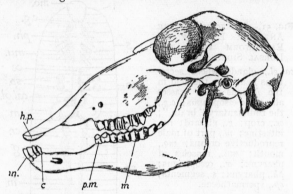

Fig. 52.—Skull of Sheep to Show Dentition. The Skull is Freshly Prepared, and the Horny Pad is Still Attached to the Upper Jaw. Canine Teeth in the Lower Jaw are Similar to the Incisors.

c., canine; *h.p.*, horny pad; *in.*, incisor; *m.*, molar; *pm.*, pre-molar.

animals that " chew the cud ". This habit may have arisen as a means of defence, for in the wild state they would have many enemies. It must have been a great convenience to be able to eat hastily, then proceed with the digestion of the food later in some place of safety.

A Sheep has no front teeth in the upper jaw. In their place is a horny pad against which it clips off grass with the teeth of the lower jaw (Fig. 52). The grass is swallowed immediately, together with a copious flow of saliva, and passes into the first division of the complicated stomach, which consists of four separate compartments.

When the animal has finished grazing it settles down to chew the cud. Food, which has become a little softened in the first two divisions of the stomach, is returned to the mouth by antiperistaltic action (p. 23). In the mouth it is thoroughly chewed and worked up with still more saliva. It is then returned to the stomach, but at this second swallowing the well-masti-

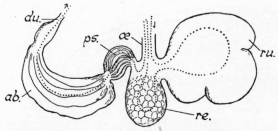

FIG. 53.—DIAGRAM OF SHEEP'S STOMACH CUT OPEN TO SHOW THE DIFFERENT CHAMBERS AND THE COURSE TAKEN BY THE FOOD.

ab., abomasum or reed; *du.*, duodenum; *œ.*, œsophagus; *ps.*, psalterium or many-plies; *re.*, reticulum or honey-bag; *ru.*, rumen.

cated food passes through the first two chambers of the stomach to the third, which acts as a filter; finally it enters the fourth chamber, which is the true stomach and secretes the gastric juices (Fig. 53).

The way in which plants build up carbohydrates from simple inorganic substances is described in Chapter VIII. This synthesis is only possible in green plants; it cannot take place in those that have no chlorophyll.

There are a few flowering plants that lack green colour. Dodder, which climbs over Gorse and other

E

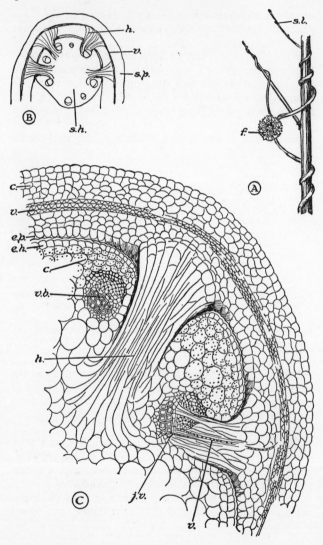

bushes on our moorlands, has no leaves at all; suckers
from its colourless stems penetrate the stems of the
Gorse or other host, and from them absorb ready-made
food (Fig. 54). Broomrape, Toothwort, and others,
which have small, colourless leaves, attach themselves to
the roots of various plants whose food-stores they tap.

Among flowerless plants that have no chlorophyll is
the great class of the Fungi, which include Mushrooms
and Toadstools, and the Moulds and Mildews. In addition there is the great army of Bacteria, which are of
such tremendous importance in the living world.

All these colourless plants get their food, as do animals,
from organic substances. Some of them, like Dodder,
Broomrape, and many of the Fungi, are *parasites*, getting their food from *living* matter; others, which are
saprophytes, take their supplies from decaying, or *non-
living*, organic substances.

Toadstools are common in woods. They live either
parasitically on the trunks or roots of trees, or sapro-
phytically on dead tree-trunks.

When a piece of beetroot, or slice of damp bread, is
left for a few days, it becomes covered with a growth of
white, silky hairs. This is the common Pin Mould. It
grows from unicellular reproductive bodies, or spores
(p. 170), which are always floating in the atmosphere.

FIG. 54.—CUSCUTA (DODDER). A, PORTION OF THE PLANT
ATTACHED TO THE STEM OF THE HOST. B, DIAGRAM OF A
TRANSVERSE SECTION OF THE STEM OF THE HOST, AND A
LONGITUDINAL SECTION OF THE STEM OF THE PARASITE. C,
SECTION OF PART OF THE STEMS MORE HIGHLY MAGNIFIED
(TRANSVERSE IN THE HOST AND LONGITUDINAL IN THE PARA-
SITE), SHOWING THE VASCULAR TISSUE OF THE HAUSTORIUM
JOINING THAT OF THE HOST.

c., cortex; *e.h.*, epidermis of host; *e.p.*, epidermis of parasite;
f., flowers; *h.*, haustorium; *j.v.*, junction of vascular tissue of
host and parasite; *s.l.*, scale leaf; *s.h.*, stem of host; *s.p.*,
stem of parasite; *v.*, vascular tissue of parasite; *v.b.*, vascular
bundle of host.

When the spores settle on the beetroot or bread, there grows out from each a thread, or filament, which takes food from the host as a result of enzyme action (p. 18). The enzymes are secreted at the tip of each filament, and act on the organic substances of the host over which the filaments spread.

Closely related to the Fungi is the unicellular plant, Yeast. A lump of Yeast is made up of a large number of single cells that multiply rapidly in a warm sugar solution. Some of the sugar is used for their growth, and some is broken down into alcohol and carbon dioxide, with release of kinetic energy. There is a rise of temperature in the sugary medium, which froths, or " ferments ", as a result of enzyme action. In the commercial use of Yeast for the manufacture of beer, germinating barley is the chief source of the sugar, and hops are added to give the desired flavour.

Among Bacteria the methods of obtaining food are very varied. Bacteria are unicellular plants, and are so small that they can only be seen by very high powers of the microscope. They are present almost everywhere, and their influence is universal. To their action the fertility of the soil is largely due; they bring about the decay of all dead matter; many cause diseases and are harmful to man.

Certain Bacteria resemble green plants in that they are able to build up a carbohydrate from the simple inorganic substances, carbon dioxide and water. Unlike green plants, they cannot get energy directly from the sun for the process; they obtain it by breaking down dead matter. They are not, therefore, as are green plants, independent of organic substances.

While it is true that plants, in general, depend on the nitrates and ammonium salts of the soil for their nitrogen supply, there are some Bacteria that are able to use free atmospheric nitrogen. They have the power of building up proteins by absorbing nitrogen from the

atmosphere. Some live freely in the soil; others are
in association with the roots of leguminous plants, such
as Clover, Lupin, Peas, and Beans, causing swellings of
the root-tissue so that conspicuous nodules are formed.
In the nodules the Bacteria live and multiply; they
use nitrogen taken from the air and carbohydrates
manufactured by their host, for the building up of

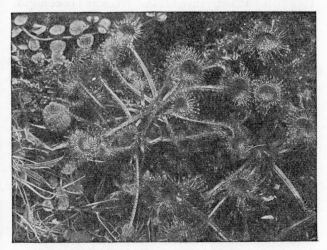

FIG. 55.—ROUND-LEAVED SUNDEW. YOUNG PLANTS
GROWING AT THE EDGE OF A BOG.

proteins (p. 76). The decay of the host-plants adds to
the nitrate-content of the soil, and this accounts for the
fact that soil is enriched by the growth of leguminous
crops.

Some green flowering plants carry on photosynthesis
in the ordinary way, but get their nitrogenous food from
other plants. Mistletoe grows generally on Apple and
Poplar trees, and from their branches it absorbs proteins
by means of penetrating suckers. Yellow Rattle and

Eyebright tap the roots of grasses for their nitrogenous food.

Other green plants which make use of nitrogenous organic compounds are the " insectivorous plants ".

From the upper surfaces of the leaves of the radical rosettes of the Sundew (*Drosera*) grow long, stalked, glandular tentacles (Fig. 55) the heads of which secrete both sticky and digestive fluids. When an insect alights

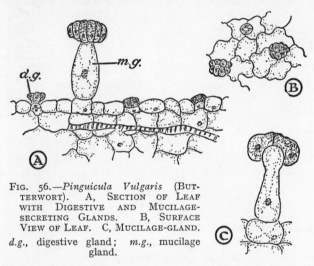

FIG. 56.—*Pinguicula Vulgaris* (BUT-
TERWORT). A, SECTION OF LEAF
WITH DIGESTIVE AND MUCILAGE-
SECRETING GLANDS. B, SURFACE
VIEW OF LEAF. C, MUCILAGE-GLAND.

d.g., digestive gland; *m.g.*, mucilage
gland.

on a leaf it is held by the sticky secretion. The tentacles it touches begin to bend over; the rest follow and the victim is completely covered. The digestive fluid, which contains enzymes, is then poured over it and it is " digested ". At the end of the process the tentacles return to their upright position; the non-digestible parts of the insect which are left are blown away by the wind or washed away by the rain.

In the Butterwort (*Pinguicula*) the mucilaginous and

digestive fluids are secreted by different glands, borne on the upper surface of the yellowish leaves of the radical rosette (Fig. 56). In this case the margins of the leaves curve over to entrap the insect, and then digestion takes place, as in the Sundew.

A very interesting insectivorous plant is the Bladder-wort (*Utricularia*). There is no evidence of the secretion of enzymes in this case. Small water-creatures are

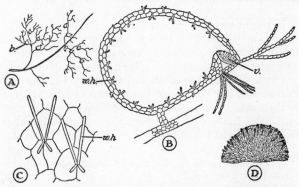

Fig. 57.—*Utricularia* (BLADDERWORT). A, PLANT WITH BLADDERS AND MUCH-DIVIDED LEAVES. B, BLADDER HIGHLY MAGNIFIED. C, FOUR-BRANCHED HAIRS ON THE INNER SURFACE OF THE BLADDER. D, VALVE FROM THE ENTRANCE TO BLADDER.

b., bladder; *v.*, valve; *w.h.*, water-absorbing hair.

entrapped in peculiar bladder-like structures; these take the place of some of the leaflets of the much-divided leaves (Fig. 57). The entrance to a bladder is guarded by a kind of valve, or trap-door, which is surrounded by hairs and only opens inwards. Water-absorbing hairs, each of which has four branches, line the inner surface of the bladder. As a result of their action both the volume of liquid and, consequently, the internal pressure in the bladder are reduced. Any slight movement of the water outside the bladder, such as might be caused by the entanglement of a small creature in the hairs around its mouth, is enough to push the trap-door inwards; then water and the captive are together swept into the trap. The resulting increased pressure in the bladder then closes the door. The captive dies and the products of decomposition are absorbed. As water is again absorbed by the lining hairs, internal pressure is once more reduced, and the whole process is repeated.

In recent years organisms have been discovered which are so small that they pass through any filter that will retain even the smallest known Bacteria. Such a " filter-passing " organism has been given the name *Virus*.

Viruses are far too small to be seen by any ordinary microscope, but their importance is out of all proportion to their size. Some of the larger viruses have been made visible by the use of invisible light; that is, by ultra-violet rays, which have a much shorter wavelength than that of visible light.

It is a moot point at present whether viruses should be classed as living things. If they are so classed they must be extremely specialised parasites, for no virus has ever been cultivated outside the living cells of its host. If power of reproducing their like be taken as a criterion of " living-ness ", then they have this property in a marked degree : the introduction of the minutest quantity of a virus into a susceptible host causes extremely rapid increase in the amount of the virus. It may be that these organisms lie on that narrow border-line which separates the non-living from the living. When viruses are extracted from their host they seem to consist of a protein of high molecular weight.

Many diseases, both of animals and plants, are due to virus-infection : measles, for instance, mumps, sleepy sickness, smallpox and rabies are some of the animal diseases caused by such infection : in the plant world it is a virus that causes the " rosette disease " of potatoes and the " mosaic disease " in the leaves of the Tobacco plant. " Witch's brooms " are often due to the same cause. Plants are often infected with virus-disease through the agency of animals : among Wallflowers, Greenflies (Aphides) spread a virus disease which produces yellow streaks in the petals of a popular blood-red strain ; when this variety of Wallflower was grown in an insect-proof greenhouse the flowers had normal petals. Such infection does not always appear to be harmful to the host plant : many of the beautiful variations in the floral leaves of the Tulip are caused by a virus ; in this case it is passed on from bulb to bulb. Virus infection seldom affects seeds, and therefore is only carried on, from one generation to another, by vegetative propagation.

CHAPTER XIV

RESPIRATION

IT is essential that all living things should breathe, in order that energy may be liberated for the carrying out of their vital functions. The mechanism of breathing may be extremely simple, or it may be highly complex as in Mammals (Ch. III). What is necessary, in all cases, is that oxygen may freely reach every part of the body.

The simplest animals live in water and depend, therefore, upon oxygen dissolved in the water of their habitat.

Unicellular animals take in dissolved oxygen over their whole surface. That *Amœba* breathes can be proved by transferring it to water that has been boiled to get rid of the air. In the new habitat the characteristic movements of the animal cease.

In simple multicellular organisms, such as *Hydra*, oxygen from the water diffuses to all cells of the body.

In larger and more complicated organisms this is not possible, because all the cells of their bodies are not in contact with the oxygen of their habitat; therefore there must be some system for the distribution of oxygen to all parts of the body.

In the Earthworm, which can only live in a damp situation, oxygen is absorbed all over the surface of the moist skin, and is then transported by a very simple blood system. It is carried by hæmoglobin as in higher animals (p. 27), but in this case the hæmoglobin is not in special blood-corpuscles, but is dissolved in the plasma of the blood.

The transport of oxygen in Insects is characteristic. It is not carried in the blood-stream, but passes along fine, branching air-tubes, or *tracheæ*, which ramify in all tissues of the body. They communicate with the atmosphere by external apertures, or spiracles (Fig. 58). Spiracles are generally obvious on the segments of a caterpillar; in the caterpillar of the Cabbage White Butterfly they appear as pairs of little black dots near the ventral surface of most of the segments. Tracheæ are strengthened internally by cartilaginous bands.

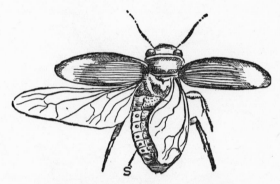

FIG. 58.—CARNIVOROUS WATER BEETLE.
Female with elytra and one wing extended showing position of spiracles; *s.*, spiracle.

By contraction of the insect's abdominal wall, air in the tracheæ is forced out through the spiracles, and fresh air then enters to take its place. The muscular contraction of the abdomen thus brings about expiration, and the flying insect is helped onward, and not retarded, by the respiratory process.

Among vertebrates Fishes are aquatic throughout their whole life; Amphibians live in water only during their early tadpole stage.

In Fishes oxygen is absorbed by the blood of special respiratory organs, the *gills*, of which there are four on either side of the back of the mouth.   Each gill consists of a bony *gill-arch*, which bears a double row of triangular *gill-filaments* on its outer edge, and tooth-like projections —*gill-rakers*—on the sides and lower part.   Between the gill-arches there are passage-ways which are open

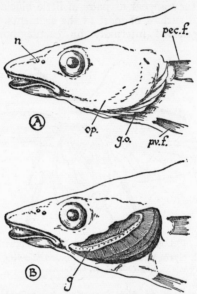

FIG. 59.—HEAD OF WHITING.

In B the operculum has been cut off to show the gills.   *g.*, gill; *g.o.*, gill-opening; *n.*, nostril; *op.*, operculum; *pec.f.*, pectoral fin; *pv.f.*, pelvic fin.

internally to the back of the mouth (the *pharynx*) and to the surrounding water externally; these open passages are the *gill-slits*.   All this can be seen on examining the head of any common fish such as Cod or Whiting (Fig. 59). In them, as in all bony fishes, the gills are covered by a stiff flap—the *operculum*—which has a flexible margin.

Water, with oxygen in solution, is taken in by way of the mouth; instead of being swallowed it is passed through the gill-slits and over the gill-filaments; the water is returned to the environment through the *gill-opening*, between the operculum and the body-wall. The respiratory interchange of gases takes place through the gill-filaments, as the water passes over them. For this reason they are richly supplied with blood, as is obvious from the pink colour of the filaments of a fresh fish. The walls both of the filaments and of the blood-capillaries are very thin, so that there is the least possible barrier between the blood-vessels and the water, from which the blood takes in oxygen, and to which it gives up carbon dioxide.

Respiration is accompanied by obvious movements. The Fish opens its mouth and, at the same time, the side walls of the pharynx press outwards against the flexible margin of the operculum, thus closing the gill-opening and enlarging the mouth-cavity, into which water is driven by external pressure. The Fish then closes both its mouth and its throat; pressure of the walls of the pharynx on the margin of the operculum is relaxed; the operculum moves slowly inwards, thus decreasing the cavity of the mouth, and water is forced out through the gill-slits and over the gill-filaments. The familiar phrase " drink like a fish " is inaccurate, for the water is used in the breathing process and not for drinking. As a matter of fact Fishes have much less need of water for drinking than have land animals, because they lose none by evaporation.

The life history of an Amphibian shows the actual transition from life in water, dependent upon the taking in of oxygen dissolved in water, to life on land dependent upon the oxygen of the atmosphere.

Frogs' eggs (p. 168) are laid in water in large numbers; each egg is enclosed in colourless jelly which swells greatly on contact with the water. Soon after a tadpole has wriggled out of the jelly, three delicate, feathery appendages—the external gills—develop on either side of its body (Fig. 60). Through them oxygen is absorbed and carbon dioxide eliminated, until a respiratory

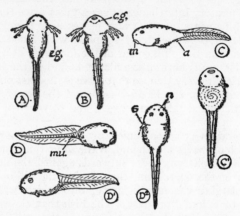

FIG. 60.—LIFE-HISTORY OF THE FROG TO THE DISAPPEAR-
ANCE OF THE EXTERNAL GILLS.

A, Tadpole from the dorsal side. Two external gills on either side. B, From the ventral side after the development of the third pair of external gills. C, C¹. C from the left side, C¹ from ventral side. Gills on right side already covered by operculum; those on left side almost enclosed. D, D¹, D². D from the right, D¹ from the left, D² from the dorsal side. External gills have disappeared and operculum has completely fused with the wall except for the " spout." *a*, anus; *c.g.*, cement gland; *e.g.*, external gills; *m.*, mouth; *mu.*, muscles of tail; *n.*, nostril; *s.*, spout.

apparatus similar to that of a Fish has developed. The external gills then disappear and the tadpole breathes like a fish, by means of internal gills, until it is about two months old when its habits change and it frequently comes to the surface of the water; this is because its lungs are developing and it needs atmospheric oxygen.

At the same time the internal gills are beginning to degenerate. During the third month of life its visits to the surface are more and more frequent, and then a distinct, and almost sudden, change takes place (Fig. 61); the tadpole becomes a Frog, which leaves the water and hops about on land. From this time onward the Frog

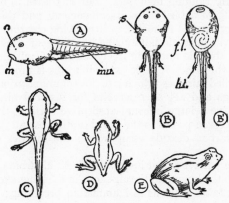

FIG. 61.—LIFE-HISTORY OF THE FROG TO THE FINAL META-MORPHOSIS.

A, Tadpole from the left side showing developing hind limb. B, B¹. B from dorsal side, B¹ from ventral side. Hind limbs further developed. Fore limbs seen beneath the operculum. C, Fore limbs free. D, Tail shortening. E, Young frog a little above life-size. *a.*, anus; *f.l.*, fore limb; *h.l.*, hind limb; *m.*, mouth; *mu.*, muscles of tail; *n.*, nostril; *s.*, spout.

is a land-breather, taking in air through its nostrils, its mouth being tightly shut except during the brief moment of catching food. Frogs are often seen squatting on water-weeds, with only their nostrils above the surface of the pond. In addition to lung-breathing, a Frog has subsidiary methods of respiration. Not all the air taken in at the nostrils passes to the lungs; some oxygen is absorbed directly by capillaries in the mucous membrane of the mouth. A Frog also breathes through its damp skin, and it soon shows signs of acute distress if its skin gets dry.

In Birds, as in Insects, respiration is adapted to the flying habit : muscular contraction brings about expiration, not inspiration, as in Mammals (p. 41). A quickly running man gets " out of breath ", but the breathing of a bird helps its movement, and this is of great importance to such a swiftly flying creature.

A Bird's lungs do not expand like those of a mammal, because they do not hang freely, but are firmly fitted in against the ribs. A large extensible area is provided by thin-walled air-sacs which are in communication with the lungs and act as reservoirs for inspired air. The lungs have a large internal absorptive surface, through which oxygen passes to the blood capillaries and through which carbon dioxide escapes into the cavities of the lungs.

In the passive act of inspiration fresh air from outside fills both the lungs and the air-sacs ; in the lungs exchange of gases takes place as in Mammalian breathing ; in expiration the air-sacs are compressed by pressure of the ribs, so that de-oxygenated air is driven out of the lungs, which then fill up with the fresh air from the air-sacs. The lungs thus receive oxygenated air both at inspiration and at expiration. That muscular contraction produces expiration, and that inspiration is the recoil, is proved by the fact that in a dead bird the air-sacs are always filled with air.

As already stated (p. 85), plants, unlike animals, have no complicated organs for the exchange and conduction of gases. Such organs are unnecessary because of the simpler structure of plants, and because their output of energy is comparatively small. Nevertheless plants, like animals, must have a constant supply of oxygen.

In the simplest plants, as in the simplest animals, the

interchange of gases takes place over the whole surface of the body, and the gases pass by diffusion from cell to cell. In the higher plants either stomata or lenticels (p. 85) usually provide the means by which the interchange of gases is effected.

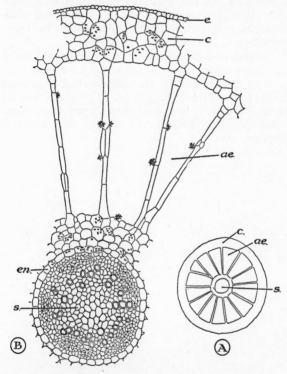

FIG. 62.—*Myriophyllum* (WATER MILFOIL). A, DIAGRAM OF TRANSVERSE SECTION OF STEM. B, TRANSVERSE SECTION OF PORTION OF STEM MORE HIGHLY MAGNIFIED.

ae., aerenchyma; *c.*, cortex; *e.*, epidermis; *en.*, endodermis; *s.*, stele.

Plants that live immersed in water, whether simple unicellular forms such as *Chlamydomonas* (p. 163) or those with leafy shoots, like the Canadian Pondweed or Water Milfoil, use oxygen from air dissolved in the water. Such plants do not lose water by evaporation and, therefore, do not need the protection of a thick cuticle : their epidermal cells are thin-walled and without stomata, and through the thin, damp walls the interchange of gases in respiration takes place.

The tissues of marsh plants, and partially submerged water-plants, often have large internal air-spaces (Fig. 62) ; they compensate for the slow method of gaseous exchange in these particular plants. The spaces also act as storage centres : the plant draws upon them when the amount of oxygen in the surrounding water is inadequate.

CHAPTER XV

MOVEMENT

ANIMALS must move in order to get their food and to escape from their enemies.

In the simplest animals movement is merely a streaming of the living protoplasm of which the organism is made up. When *Amœba* (p. 123) is mounted on a slide in a drop of water, and examined under the microscope, it is seen to change its shape. Protoplasm streams from the central mass, pushing out in one or more directions; the rest of the mass follows, with the result that the animal moves onward.

Such simple movement is possible only in a unicellular organism. In all multicellular animals movement is brought about by special cells which have the power of altering their shape, becoming long and thin or, alternatively, short and thick. These are the muscle-cells, and it is by their contraction and expansion that movement is brought about.

Hydra, the Water Polyp (p. 125), is a simple multicellular animal. It is usually stationary and attached to the stem of a water plant. Because it gets its food from the surrounding water it moves very little from place to place. It does, however, move considerably *in situ*, alternately elongating and shortening. When fully extended it may be more than half an inch in length and plainly visible to the naked eye; upon contraction it becomes a roundish knob.

The body-wall of *Hydra* is made up of two layers of cells. Those of the outer layer have extensions, or muscle-tails, arranged *parallel* to its length (Fig. 50); the contraction of these muscle-tails makes the animal short and thick. Similar muscle-tails of the cells of the inner layer are *at right angles* to the length of the body; on their contraction the body becomes long and thin.

Occasionally *Hydra* moves from one fixed spot to another. It may swim through the water by means of its tentacles, or it may advance by a series of somersaults. More frequently it progresses by " looping ", when the body curves until its free end touches a more distant part of the support which is gripped by the tentacles; the fixed basal end then relaxes its hold and moves in a straight line until it reaches the tentacles; here it becomes fixed once more and the tentacles let go their hold. By repetition of this activity *Hydra* moves forward.

In animals of greater complexity large numbers of contracting cells are closely associated, forming definite muscle-tissue.

In the body-wall of the Earthworm there are two layers of muscle-tissue. The outer layer consists of *circular* muscles which contract at right angles to the length of the worm, thus making it long and thin; those of the inner layer are *longitudinal*—that is, parallel to the worm's length—and when they contract the animal shortens and thickens.

The Earthworm, unlike *Hydra*, must progress in order to get food. On the lower surface of each of its segments there are four pairs of bristles which point backwards, and are felt when the under-surface is stroked from the posterior to the anterior end. They are plainly seen when the animal is held up to the light.

In progression a worm grips the soil with the bristles of the posterior and anterior segments alternately. In the first position the soil is gripped by the posterior bristles and the rest of the body is raised from the ground and elongated. The anterior bristles are then fixed in the soil; and the rest of the body is raised and contracted. When the bristles are again fixed the new

position is established.   If an Earthworm is placed on
a smooth surface, such as a piece of glass, it can get no
grip; it makes wriggling contortions, but there is no
progression.

The movement of the Com-
mon Snail depends upon the
contractions of a muscular mass
of tissue which is called the
" foot " by virtue of its function, and which is on the ventral side of the body.   If a
Snail is put on a piece of glass
it can be held upside down,
because the mucous substance
it secretes makes it adhere to
the glass.   Muscular contrac-

FIG. 63.—THE FRESH-
WATER SHRIMP.

tions are then seen to pass, like a series of waves, from
the posterior to the anterior end of the foot.

Arthropods are higher in the scale of life and have

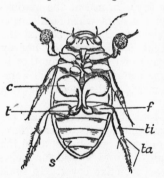

FIG. 64.—CARNIVOROUS
WATER BEETLE.

Ventral aspect of male insect.
c., coxa; *f.*, femur; *s.*, sternum; *t.*, trochanter; *ta.*,
tarsus; *ti.*, tibia.

special paired and *jointed*
appendages (p. 176).   The
largest number of appen-
dages occurs in the Crus-
taceans (Fig. 63).   In some
of them, as in the Cray-
fish, Lobster, and Shrimp,
certain appendages are
used for other purposes,
as well as for swimming.

Spiders   progress   on
land by means of four pairs
of long, seven-jointed legs.

Insects have three pairs
of legs.   These are five-
jointed, and are used for
progression on land or in
water.

Some Insects are powerful swimmers. The third pair of legs of the Great Water Beetle, a common inhabitant of our ponds, are beautifully adapted to this end. Their movement is like a sculling stroke. The last two joints, the *tibia* and *tarsus*, are flattened and fringed on one side with stiff hairs (Fig. 64), which are spread out while the leg is making the stroke, and depressed during the return. The tarsus rotates a little on its own axis, enabling the beetle to " feather " its natural oar. The smooth, polished surface of the limbs and of the entire body reduces friction and thus is an aid to rapid movement in the water. Another powerful insect-swimmer is the Water Boatman.

Insects differ from all other Invertebrates in being able to fly. In addition to legs for progression on land and in water, they have, at least during one stage of their life-history, wings for use in the air. Flight may serve for the purpose of getting food, as in the case of Butterflies, Bees, and Moths, that all take nectar from flowers. Sometimes wings are only fully formed at the mating-time, as in the nuptial flights of Ants, when fertilization takes place at a great height in the air, beyond the range of sight. Insects that live in water do not fly much; sometimes they leave one pond for another in search of a mate. In some instances, as in the Common Cockroach, only the males of the species develop wings.

Two pairs of wings are typical of insects. They are borne dorsally on the thorax which, on its under surface, bears also the three pairs of legs. Sometimes, as in the Water Beetle, only one pair of wings is used for flight, and the other pair forms a protective cover. In some insects only one pair of wings is developed.

In the lowest class of Vertebrates, the Fishes, movement through the water is brought about by the strong muscles of the body and tail. A fish is extremely muscular; there is more flesh in the body of a fish than in any other animal of equal size. The need for such exceptional muscular development is explained by the great activity of fishes, by the environment in which they live, and by their surprising migrations.

In a steak of Salmon, Hake, or any other large fish, it is plainly seen that the muscles are segmented, and that each mass of muscle is V-shaped.

Because Fishes have to move swiftly in a heavy medium, it is essential that their form and surface should be such as to minimize friction and impede

FIG. 65.—DIAGRAM TO ILLUSTRATE SHAPE OF FISH AND PRESSURE OF WATER ON ITS SURFACE.

movement as little as possible. To this end a free-swimming fish is shaped like a double wedge. The anterior wedge is short and the posterior one long, thus

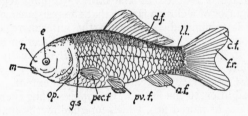

FIG. 66.—GOLDFISH.

a.f., anal fin; *c.f.*, caudal fin; *d.f.*, dorsal fin; *e.*, eye,; *f.r.*, fin ray; *g.s.*, gill-opening; *l.l.*, lateral line; *m.*, mouth; *n.*, nares; *op.*, operculum; *pec.f.*, pectoral fin; *pv.f.*, pelvic fin.

the widest part is behind the head. The pressure of the water acts at right angles to the surface of the body and is proportional to its area. Therefore, as is seen on referring to Fig. 65, quite a slight muscular effort is enough to drive a fish forward. No projecting parts and no neck break the continuity of the outline. The surface is smooth and slimy and is protected by an armour of scales, which in no way hamper progress because they are flat and point backwards.

Balance in the water is maintained and movement is directed by the fins, which are formed from expanded folds of the body-wall and are supported by fin-rays. In the median plane there are one or more *dorsal* fins, a tail, or *caudal*, fin which is typically two-lobed, and a ventral, or *anal*, fin (Fig. 66). The dorsal and anal fins serve to keep the fish upright in the water, with the dorsal side uppermost. That some effort is needed to maintain this position is evident from the fact that a dead fish floats with the ventral side uppermost, and the head at a lower level than the tail.

The caudal fin acts in conjunction with the muscles of the tail to bring about movement. To effect this the tail curves a little to one side; at the same time the fin-surface is reduced by the fin-rays coming together like the ribs of a closing fan, so that the resistance of the water is minimized. Meanwhile the anterior region of the body curves slightly in the opposite direction to the tail. In the swimming stroke the tail is rapidly and forcefully straightened against the pressure of the water and the fin-surface is expanded to its full extent.

In addition to the median, or unpaired, fins there are two pairs of paired fins, which foreshadow the limbs of higher Vertebrates. These are the *pectoral* and *pelvic* fins, which project like shelves, help the fish to keep its balance, and are particularly useful for steering, as they act independently on either side. Sometimes, as in the Stickleback, they are powerful organs of propulsion.

The Eel is an example of a very powerful swimmer. The whole body may be regarded as a swimming organ, because it acts like a long tail. Such powerful movement is necessary because of the long journeys taken by Eels to reach their breeding ground; they are born in the sea, and return to it when they reach maturity.

The fascinating life-history of the Eel has been a

mystery for centuries. As late as 1653 Izaak Walton writes that " Eels are bred of a particular dew falling about May or June on the banks of ponds and rivers ". Even up to the present time no female with mature eggs has been seen, nor have the newly laid eggs been discovered. A great deal of the story is, however, now known.

Every year in May and June young Eels, or " elvers ", come to the mouths of our rivers in countless numbers. They swim up-stream, penetrating to every little pool. They live in fresh water for several years, and during that time they eat enormously, causing great destruction among the river population.

After a certain time, perhaps between the ages of 7 and 10, some instinct recalls them to the sea. They travel down the rivers, often making short cuts across land, and when they have reached the sea they swim westwards. The journey is full of peril from sharks and other large sea fishes. Those Eels that survive finally reach their breeding ground in the deep waters of the western Atlantic.

Here, not far from the Bermudas, countless throngs of Eels, both from the Old World and the New, meet every year from early spring to late summer. The journey has been long and exhausting, and it is probable that the fish die after breeding. In their stead are countless millions of tiny, transparent, leaf-like creatures, which set off on their long journey " home ". Those of western parentage head west for America; the Europeans travel east. It is a three years' journey to Europe, and the proportion of survivors is small; still it is enough to produce the swarms of elvers that reach our shores each year.

During their journey across the Atlantic the young Eels lose their leaf-like shape and assume the snake-like form of the mature fish. The American Eels have a shorter distance to travel and it takes them only a year to reach their rivers; they mature more quickly than the European Eels.

The movement of Amphibians in their early stages is similar to that of Fishes, because they, too, live in water. A tadpole has no fins, but its tail is long and fin-like and acts as a swimming organ. Through the skin of the tail >-shaped markings are clearly seen, indicating muscle segments similar to those of a Fish.

As a tadpole develops it gradually changes from an animal adapted for life in water to one adapted for life on land. When tadpoles finally leave the water their tails have completely disappeared and from now onwards the movement of a Frog depends entirely on two pairs of limbs of the pentadactyl type (p. 47).

The Frog is a strong swimmer; on land it progresses by a series of leaps. Its fore-limbs are short and consist of three parts—the arm, fore-arm, and hand—and terminate in four digits. The first digit, corresponding to the thumb of Man, is rudimentary; the third finger is the longest. When a Frog is swimming these limbs lie flat against the sides of the body. On land they are useful for slow movements; they are also used for alighting after a leap, and for raising the anterior end of the body, both when the animal is at rest and when it is preparing to jump.

The hind-limbs are the chief organs of movement, both on land and in water. Like the fore-limbs, they are made up of three parts—the thigh, the leg, and the foot—and they also terminate in digits. They are much longer than the fore-limbs : the thigh and leg are twice as long as the arm and fore-arm, and the ankle and foot are four times the length of the wrist and hand. There are five well developed toes; the shortest is that which corresponds to the big toe of man; the fourth is the longest. The toes are webbed, thus increasing the efficiency of the limb as a swimming-organ. In preparing for a leap the three parts of the leg are stretched out into a straight line.

The higher classes of Vertebrates are terrestrial animals moving on the surface of the earth, or in the air. A few, like the Whale and the Seal, have reverted to water.

Among Reptiles the Snakes have developed a gliding motion, directed by the strong body-muscles and by the movement of the large number of ribs which are in connection with all vertebræ except the most anterior. Such movement would be greatly hampered by lateral appendages, and they are lacking. Traces of hind-limbs still persist under the skin of certain Snakes, notably in the Python, indicating that remote Snake-ancestors had such appendages. During countless ages Snakes have become adapted to their particular mode of life by the disappearance of limbs, which would be not merely useless to them but definitely a drawback.

Of all the special modifications of the fore-limbs of Vertebrates the most interesting is that which occurs in Birds, where the fore-limb is converted into a wing. The habits and characteristics of Birds are intimately connected with this modification of the fore-limb. Migration is possible to them because they can use their wings for long-distance flights. The migratory habit enables them to circumvent winter hardships; on the approach of autumn, when food is becoming scarce, many travel southward, and return to the north once more with returning spring.

In the garden, in early summer, one may pick up a young sparrow that has died by falling from its nest. Such a young bird is useful for the study of the wing (Fig. 67), because the feathers which cover it later are not fully developed. The three parts of the wing cannot be brought into a straight line, even when it is stretched to its full extent. This is prevented by two folds of skin, one stretching across the bend of the elbow, the other across the arm-pit. The bones of the individual digits, and those of the palm and wrist, are fused together; the thumb, only, is separate, appearing as a little knob.

Such fusion gives firm support for the powerful flight-feathers. These are the *quill*-feathers, and are borne on the lower edge of the fore-arm and hand. Their number is constant for any one species. The bases of the quills are connected by a delicate elastic band that prevents their displacement with reference to each other,

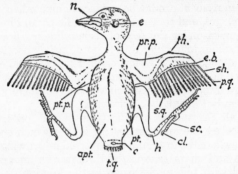

FIG. 67.—A NESTLING SPARROW.

apt., apteria; *c.*, cloaca; *cl.*, claw; *e.*, ear tube; *e.b.*, elastic band; *h.*, heel; *n.*, nostril; *p.q.*, primary quill; *pr.p.*, propatagium; *pt.p.*, postpatagium; *pt.*, pterylæ; *sc.*, scales on foot; *sh.*, sheath of quill-feather; *s.q.*, secondary quill; *th.*, thumb feathers; *t.q.*, quill-feathers of tail.

and brings the quill-feathers back into position after the wing has been extended. The wing of the nestling is naked except for the developing quill-feathers; later it becomes clothed with *covert*, or " covering ", feathers.

A quill-feather consists of a central axis, and a blade-like, expanded portion—the *vane*. The axis is made up of a hollow *quill* and a solid, upper part—the *shaft*. The vane looks like one continuous sheet, but a slight pull is sufficient to make an oblique rent in it. After making such a rent, if the vane is pressed gently upwards and outwards between the finger and thumb, the injury can be completely " mended ". This is possible because the vane is made up of separate parts, termed *barbs*, which are borne on the shaft somewhat in the manner of teeth on a comb, except that they are oblique and occur on both sides of the axis. The barbs are branched on both sides, and the branches of successive barbs are linked together by hooks and flanges.

The quill-feathers of the hand form the cutting edge of the wing in flight; they are of great use for steering and for changing direction in the horizontal plane. The quill feathers of the fore-arm seem to be more important for the actual stroke.

The movement of the wings in flight is as complicated as it is beautiful. They are first raised to an almost vertical position in which they are brought right over the back; sometimes they even strike audibly, one against the other. They then cut the air forward and downward. After this they move backward and upward again. During the complete circuit the tip moves through a double loop.

The movements depend upon the strong muscles of the breast. These are exceptionally well developed and account, on an average, for about one-sixth of the entire weight of the bird. The " breast " and the keeled bone— the *sternum*—to which it is attached are familiar to all who have carved birds that are used for food. Two muscles on each side of the sternum make up the breast. Although the two muscles of each side are attached to the same bone, one serves to raise the wing, the other to lower it. The outer, larger muscle on each side is directly attached by its tendon to the under side of the bone of the arm (the humerus), and by its contraction the wing is lowered. The second smaller and inner muscle passes, by means of its tendon, through an aperture in the shoulder-joint and is attached to the humerus on its upper side; the contraction of this muscle, therefore, raises the wing.

Some understanding of the forces which act on the wing during flight may be gained by a consideration of the parallelogram of forces. The wing is brought downward by the action of the powerful breast-muscles against the resistance of the air. This resistance has a greater effect on the hinder, flexible part than on the front rigid portion of the wing and, as a consequence, the wing takes an oblique position. The resistant force of the air, which acts at right angles to the plane of the wing, can be resolved into vertical and horizontal components; the vertical component tends to buoy the bird up, and the horizontal component to carry it forward. Flight is not, of course, such a simple matter as this. The varying convexities of the wing and other important factors have to be taken into account.

When the wing is brought downward it acts as one large expanded plane, impermeable to air. The quill-feathers are kept in position by the stretched elastic band at their bases, which are protected by covert-feathers, so that no air gets through. The interlocking of the barbs makes the vanes, also, impenetrable. Increase in wing surface is produced by the stretching of the membranes between the joints of the arm, and a very efficient " plane " is thus produced.

As the wing is brought upwards for the next stroke the elastic band relaxes, thus allowing the air to slip between the feathers, and the area of the wing is reduced; resistance is still further lessened owing to the convex shape of the upper surface, which enables the air to slip off it easily.

Flight is assisted by the action of the feathers of the tail. The tail of a bird is a mere stump on which quill-feathers are arranged in a horizontal plane, their bases being covered and protected by covert-feathers. The quill-feathers move independently of one another in the horizontal plane, so that the tail can spread out fan-wise. The tail also moves as a whole in the vertical plane.

The functions of the tail are to preserve balance and also to steer in the vertical plane. A bird that has lost its tail-feathers can still fly, but does so erratically; it finds it difficult to ascend and descend at will. When a bird " cocks " its tail during flight, the air from the down-stroke of the wing strikes it underneath and it descends; if, on the other hand, the tail is depressed the air strikes it above and the bird rises.

The hind limbs of birds are of the pentadactyl type; they are used for progression on land and in water. The toes, which terminate in claws, are never more than four in number. A bird walks on its toes, the rest of the foot being raised above the ground. Generally in perching-birds the big toe is directed backward and the other three forward. The feet and legs of birds are indicative of their habits. Strong swimmers like the Duck have webbed feet. Wading birds like the Heron have very long legs and feet, and spreading toes which give a large base for support.

In Mammals, the highest group of Vertebrates, progression is, with one exception, either on land or in the water; this exception is the family of the Bats, which alone have conquered the air.

Almost invariably the hind-limbs of Mammals are used for progression in some manner, but the fore-limbs have, in many cases, been adapted to other uses; more especially is this the case in the arm of Man.

Quickly moving animals run on their toes and have the wrist and ankle raised high above the ground. This is true of the Horse and is outstandingly the case in the Giraffe.

Interesting modifications of limb-structure have taken place among aquatic Mammals, where the limbs are used for progression in water. In Sea Lions, Seals, and Walrus they are converted into stout, fin-like flippers, while their bodies tend to be fish-like in shape, being long, lithe, and without a neck. Modification has gone still further in the Whale and Porpoise; they are even more fish-like in appearance, for they have a dorsal fin and a forked tail; their fore-limbs are converted into swimming-paddles and the hind-limbs are missing altogether.

In the wing of the Bat more has been sacrificed to flight than in the wing of the Bird, for the bones of both hind- and fore-limb are enclosed in the covering of skin which forms the wing. On the ground the Bat can do no more than just shuffle along.

Monkeys use the hind-limbs more than the fore-limbs for progression. The tail-less Apes never go completely on all-fours; the Gibbon, indeed, walks erect, but only with the help of his immensely long arms, which actually reach the ground.

In Man alone is progression entirely dependent upon the hind-limbs, for Man alone has entirely assumed the upright attitude.

As plants are surrounded by their food-building materials, they need not, like animals, move about in search of food. Consequently, they are generally speaking, rooted to one spot. This rooting is necessary to give stability and, at the same time, to enable the plants to absorb solutions from the soil.

Even plants that live in water may have a fixed position. The Bladderwrack (p. 166) adheres firmly to rocks, so that it may not be torn by waves and currents. Fresh-water weeds are often rooted in the muddy bed of the pond or stream.

Motility is not, however, entirely an animal characteristic. Very simple plants swim about in the water in which they live. Among unicellular organisms, seen under the microscope in a drop of pond-water, some are green and have an enclosing wall. These are very simple plants. *Chlamydomonas* (p. 163) is one of the most common; it is pear-shaped and swims by means of two long threads of protoplasm, or *flagella*, which are at its pointed end.

Among multicellular plants there is no motility of the plant as a whole; it occurs only in the active swimming of the male cells, or *spermatozoids*. Non-Flowering Plants that reproduce sexually all have spermatozoids. Those of Bladderwrack are set free from the plant, and swim, by means of two flagella, to the egg-cells which have floated out into the water (p. 167). Such motile male-cells are characteristic, too, of Ferns and Mosses (p. 170). Only in Flowering-Plants has the motility of the male cell been entirely lost; it is carried to the egg-cell by the pollen-tube, which grows down through the style of a flower, after the pollen-grain has been deposited on its stigma (p. 102).

F

CHAPTER XVI

REPRODUCTION

In order that the various species of living things may continue in existence, it is necessary for the members of one generation to produce their like before they die. The continuance of the species is of such vital importance that Nature is improvident and wasteful in the production of new individuals, so that some, at least, may have the right conditions for survival. " So careful of the type she seems, so careless of the single life."

The Eel is one instance of Nature's prodigality : it has been calculated that, in the ovary of a female 32 inches long, the number of eggs is 10,700,000 !

The simplest possible method of reproduction occurs in some unicellular organisms. *Amœba*, when it has reached a certain size, divides into two individuals which separate, grow to the size of the parent, and, in due time, themselves divide into two. Division takes place in the following way : the nucleus lengthens and becomes constricted in the middle; the surrounding protoplasm accommodates itself to the changed shape of the nucleus, so that the animal becomes dumb-bell shaped; finally there is an actual break at the constriction, so that two *Amœbæ* now exist where previously there was only one (Fig. 49). But not only has the number of individuals increased—there has, at the same time, been some mysterious rejuvenation of the protoplasm that produces, in place of one old *Amœba*, two young ones.

The earliest living things probably reproduced in some such way as this. The method is efficient so far as the production of an ever-increasing number of individuals is concerned; but as the new organisms are simply halves of pre-existing individuals, they cannot have any character that the parent did not possess, except in so far as they may be influenced by changes in their environment. There is little scope for variation in such a reproductive method.

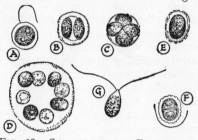

FIG. 68.—*CHLAMYDOMONAS EHRENBERGH.*

A–D, Stages in asexual reproduction. E, Zygote. F, Zygote dividing. G, Young vegetative individual produced by division of zygote. (After Goroschankin.)

In the great majority of plants and animals two individuals play a part in reproduction. As their offspring inherit qualities from two parents, instead of from one only as in *Amœba*, there are possibilities of variation in each succeeding generation.

Chlamydomonas, being a plant, is surrounded by a cell-wall. It reproduces, as does *Amœba*, by division into two. These two cells may in their turn

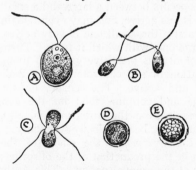

FIG. 69.—*CHLAMYDOMONAS REINHARDI,* SEXUAL REPRODUCTION OF SIMILAR GAMETES.

A, Vegetative individual. B, Gametes. C, Conjugation of gametes. D, Young zygote. E, Ripe zygote. (After Goroschankin.)

divide, forming four or eight individuals within the wall of the parent-cell (Fig. 68). Soon the wall of the "mother"-cell ruptures and the "daughters" swim away.

Chlamydomonas has also a second method of reproduction, in which several divisions take place inside the parent, resulting in eight, sixteen, thirty-two, or even sixty-four tiny cells. By the rupture of the parent-wall these cells are set free and swim out into the water, where they meet similar cells that have originated from another parent (Fig. 69). Two cells, of different ancestry, swim towards one another, their anterior ends come into contact and, finally, they unite completely. Here is seen the foreshadowing of the sexual process, which has become the stereotyped method of reproduction in higher plants and animals.

Sexual differentiation is carried a step farther in one species of *Chlamydomonas*, in which some individuals produce only a few large daughter-cells, while others give rise to a large number of small ones. When fusion takes place it always occurs between a large and a small cell. The large one is less active, and may even remain motionless in the water; the small one is very active, and swims to the large one, with which it fuses. There is thus, in a member of this primitive group of living things, a differentiation of sex characters. The male individual is small and active. The female, on the other hand, is large and contains food for the new individuals which result from the fusion; it is, also, only feebly motile, and may be completely stationary.

In *Amœba* and *Chlamydomonas* the whole of the organism is used up in the production of the offspring; there is nothing left of the original parent. This costly method is inevitable in unicellular individuals. In multicellular organisms reproduction is the work of certain specialized cells only, while the rest are concerned with other activities. This is an economy in the use of material, and also enables the parent to go on living after producing offspring.

The two cells which unite in fertilization—that is the *gametes*—differ in character. The male gametes are very small and, except in Flowering Plants, they are motile, swimming by the lashing of one or more protoplasmic threads, or *flagella*. It is their work to reach the stationary female cell, or *ovum*, which in many

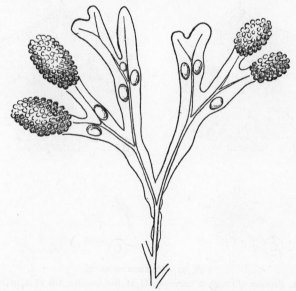

FIG. 70.—FUCUS, THE BLADDERWRACK.

animals stores food for the early growth of the new individual.

Hydra produces male and female cells on the same individual at the same time. The male gametes, or *sperms*, develop in the *testis* which is situated just below the tentacles (Fig. 50). Within it develop a large number of minute sperms, which swim by means of a long flagellum when they are set free. The female organ—the *ovary*—is near the base, and in it only one egg develops. This is not liberated, but the ovary wall that encloses it becomes gelatinous, and sperms, generally from another *Hydra*, attack this gelatinous envelope; eventually one penetrates and fuses with the ovum. The embryo that results from the fusion begins to develop *in situ* so

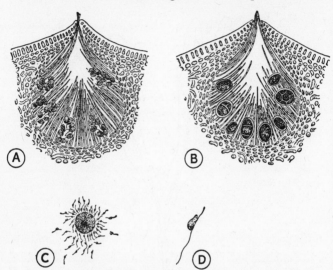

FIG. 71.—BLADDERWRACK.

A, Section through a conceptacle at the swollen tip of a male plant. B, Section through a conceptacle at the swollen tip of a female plant. C, Oosphere surrounded by spermatozoids. D, Single spermatozoid.

that, for a time, some slight protection is afforded by the parent. Soon, however, it becomes detached, and its development is completed in the mud at the bottom of the pond.

In Bladderwrack (Fig. 70) the eggs of the plant are fertilized by male gametes, as in *Hydra*. In this familiar

brown sea-weed, however, the two kinds of sexual cells
are borne on different individuals. Bladderwrack forks
repeatedly, and the ends of the branches are swollen.
Numerous small dots seen on the swollen ends are pores
that lead into pits in which the gametes (oospheres and
spermatozoids) are formed (Fig. 71).

When the gametes are mature they are extruded into
the water with a mucilaginous substance which is olive-
green in the female and orange-coloured in the male.
The spermatozoids swim actively by the lashing of two
flagella. The egg-cells (oospheres), which are stationary,
are much larger than the spermatozoids, because they
store food. When the spermatozoids and eggs are put
together in a drop of salt water and looked at under a
microscope, the spermatozoids are seen to surround the
egg-cell, which must, therefore, attract them in some
way. Such an attraction is a constant and necessary
factor in sexual reproduction.

In the Earthworm, as in *Hydra*, both kinds of sexual
organs are present in one individual, although *self*-
fertilization does not take place, and some of the
characteristics of two separate worms are present in the
offspring.

As Earthworms live on land, the character of the
environment makes it impossible for the gametes to
unite unless the individuals that produce them meet in
pairs. On warm, summer mornings, pairing Earthworms
are often seen on a lawn. Two worms lie with their
anterior ventral portions close together, while their
posterior ends may still be within their respective
burrows. Sperms, which are set free through apertures
in the ventral surface of each worm, are exchanged and
stored, and the worms then separate.

On a mature worm, at about a third of its length
from the front end, there is a swollen ring which secretes
a mucous substance. A band of this mucus becomes
loose after pairing has taken place; the worm then

wriggles backwards, so that the band is passed towards the head. As it slips forward it receives eggs, which pass out through two apertures on the ventral side of the worm's body; when it has moved still farther forward it collects the stored sperms previously received from the other worm that was concerned in the act of pairing. As soon as the ring has passed over the Earthworm's head it hardens and, because of its elasticity, it closes up at both ends forming a cocoon. Within this cocoon one or more of the eggs are fertilized, but generally only one develops; no provision is made by the parents for the care of the young worm.

The instinctive habits of many insects lead to " aftercare " of their offspring. The Cabbage White Butterfly, for example, lays her eggs on the leaves of the cabbage, or of some other plant of the family Cruciferæ, and these are suitable food for the caterpillars when they emerge.

Little or no care for their offspring is shown by Fishes, Amphibians, and Reptiles. In the warm-blooded Vertebrates the strength of the bond between parent and offspring is an outstanding characteristic.

The eggs of some Fishes are not fertilized until they are in the water; in others fertilization takes place in the body of the female. In either case, with some few exceptions, the fertilized eggs are extruded by the female, so that further development takes place in the water. Apart from the storage of " yolk " in the egg there is no parental responsibility.

Frogs mate early in Spring, and return to the ponds for this purpose. The male rests on the back of the female, clasping her tightly under the arm-pits by means of his " thumb- " pads. They remain in this position for several days. In swimming, leaping into the air, or darting for food, they move as one. In due time the female extrudes her eggs, which are fertilized immediately by sperms shed over them by the male. As

soon as spawning is accomplished the male releases his
hold of the female and takes no further notice of her.
Neither does either of the parents take any interest in
the tadpoles which are, however, provided with food,
or yolk, for their initial development, and which are
given their start in life in a suitable environment.

Such external fertilization is only possible when eggs
are deposited in water and can be reached by sperms
that swim in the water. It is quite impossible for
land-animals, and therefore internal fertilization—that is,
fertilization within the body of the female—is the general
rule among more highly developed organisms. Internal
fertilization, and the consequent connection between
the mother and her offspring, is the basis of parental
care in the animal world.

As the fertilized eggs of Birds are deposited on land,
they need some protection—hence the egg-shell. When
the egg is laid it is not neglected, but is kept warm
during the development of the embryo. For this
development an ample store of yolk is necessary because
a Bird reaches quite an advanced stage of development
before it pecks its way out of the shell; even then its
parents continue to look after it and provide it with
food. Thus, side by side with the increasing care shown
by parents, is seen the greater helplessness of the young.

Primitive Mammals, such as the Duck-billed Platypus,
lay their eggs as Birds and Reptiles do. In all higher
Mammals the egg is not set free after fertilization, but
develops within the body of the mother. There is
organic connection between the mother and the developing embryo. By this means food in solution and
oxygen for respiration pass from parent to offspring.
Even after birth a new-born Mammal is still dependent
on its mother for nourishment, for all suckle their young
with milk from the mammary glands.

In plants, as in animals, the transition from life in
water to life on land is accompanied by the retention of

the egg-cell within the parent. Mosses and Ferns are reproduced by the fertilization *in situ* of egg-cells by spermatozoids which swim to them through the water. The parent plant provides protection for the fertilized egg, and food for its development. In Flowering Plants still greater provision is made for the new individual (Chap. XI); the fertilized egg remains protected and fed by the parent plant until the embryo is fully formed.

Many plants are reproduced *asexually*. In the great class of the Fungi such asexual reproduction is general.

In the common Pin Mould, seen on damp bread or beetroot (p. 131), vertical white threads, an inch or so long, grow from the branching filaments that cover the surface of the host. The ends of the threads swell forming globular heads, which are first white, but later turn black. Under the microscope they are seen to be thin-walled cases, containing numbers of minute cells called *spores*. When a case ruptures the spores are set free in clouds. On a suitable medium they germinate and give rise to a new generation of the mould.

Similar spores are produced on the " caps " of Mushrooms and Toadstools. They are borne on structures called *gills*, which radiate from the centre to the circumference on the under side of the head. To see the spores the cap should be cut off and laid with the gills downwards on a piece of clean paper, and covered with a tumbler to prevent evaporation. By the following day the spores will have fallen, making a beautiful pattern of the radiating gills.

Asexual spores occur in spore-cases that form the brown masses on the backs of Ferns, and are produced also in the little capsules of Mosses.

Yet another method of reproduction among plants is *vegetative propagation*. This depends neither on sexually produced seeds nor on asexually produced spores, for a new plant just grows from a part of the old one. It sometimes happens that plants that multiply vegetatively lose the power of producing seeds; this is the explanation of the seedless condition of the Banana.

In vegetative propagation some portion of the parent plant becomes detached and develops independently. In this way rapid multiplication of plants is brought about. Familiar structures concerned in such propagation are *suckers* (Rose), *tubers* (Potato), *bulbs* (Hyacinth), *bulbils* (Onion), *corms* (Crocus), *rhizomes* (Iris), and *runners* (Strawberry).

In such a method of multiplication there is little possibility of variation in the offspring. This is one of its advantages from the gardener's point of view, because it is possible to be sure beforehand of the characteristics of plants that are produced in this way.

CHAPTER XVII

CLASSIFICATION

OVER almost the whole surface of the earth, and throughout the waters of the sea, life of some sort abounds. Its range and variety are infinite; it exists in tropical jungles and in ice-bound arctic regions; it may be in the form of a highly developed vertebrate animal, with a separate and complex organ responsible for each individual function, or it may be nothing more than a minute mass of protoplasm that, within its extremely limited scope, is able to carry out all vital functions.

Animals are primarily classed in two great groups—the *Vertebrates* and the *Invertebrates* (Fig. 72).

All Vertebrates are characterized by having an internal skeleton made up of a spine and, except in the case of Fishes, two pairs of limbs of the pentadactyl type.

The five classes of Vertebrates are Fish, Amphibians, Reptiles, Birds, and Mammals.

The highly organized structure of a Mammal, the highest of the Vertebrate group, is exemplified in the Rabbit.

Of the other classes of Vertebrates the most primitive are the Fishes. They still live in their ancestral habitat, and for breathing use oxygen from air dissolved in the surrounding water; they do not need, and have not developed, the pentadactyl limbs characteristic of the other four classes.

Amphibians, which include Frogs, Newts, and Toads, pass the early stages of their life in water breathing as Fishes do. This is their tadpole stage. Later their lungs develop and they leave the water for life on land. Amphibians, like all the higher Vertebrates, have two

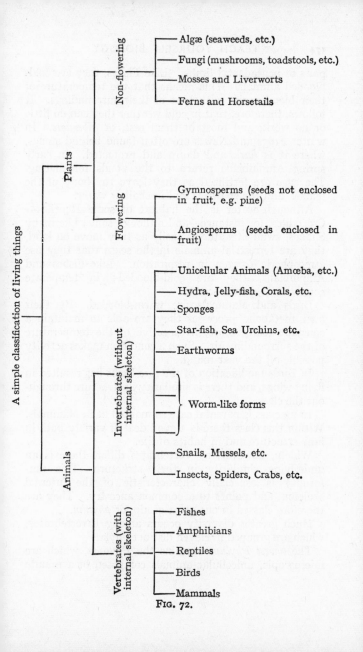

A simple classification of living things

Plants
- Non-flowering
  - Algæ (seaweeds, etc.)
  - Fungi (mushrooms, toadstools, etc.)
  - Mosses and Liverworts
  - Ferns and Horsetails
- Flowering
  - Gymnosperms (seeds not enclosed in fruit, e.g. pine)
  - Angiosperms (seeds enclosed in fruit)

Animals
- Invertebrates (without internal skeleton)
  - Unicellular Animals (Amœba, etc.)
  - Hydra, Jelly-fish, Corals, etc.
  - Sponges
  - Star-fish, Sea Urchins, etc.
  - Earthworms
  - Worm-like forms
  - Snails, Mussels, etc.
  - Insects, Spiders, Crabs, etc.
- Vertebrates (with internal skeleton)
  - Fishes
  - Amphibians
  - Reptiles
  - Birds
  - Mammals

FIG. 72.

pairs of pentadactyl limbs. Like Fishes, they are cold-blooded animals. This means that the temperature of their blood varies with that of their surroundings. It follows, therefore, that in cold weather they can do little or no work, and most of them rest, or *hibernate*. In winter Frogs and Newts are often found behind stones, where it is dark and damp and protected. In early spring Amphibians return to the ponds for mating. The eggs are fertilized as they leave the body of the female, and the spawn is laid in shallow water.

Although water is the habitat of some Reptiles—Crocodiles, for instance—and although some, like many Snakes, swim in water as easily as they move on land, they are terrestrial animals in the sense that they use atmospheric oxygen in respiration. Like Fishes and Amphibians, they are cold-blooded; in temperate countries they are scarce.

Birds and Mammals are warm-blooded. By their own metabolic processes they are able to maintain a constant temperature, irrespective of the temperature of the surrounding air. Such a condition makes activity possible all the year round.

In Birds modification of the fore-limbs has resulted in flying wings, and there is similarity in structure throughout the class.

In no class is parental care so marked as in Mammals. Within this class there is a good deal of variety both in limb-structure and in habits of life.

Widely, however, as Vertebrates differ, there is an underlying similarity in their structure. This uniformity is especially characteristic of the internal skeleton, and points to a common ancestry. They are therefore classed in one great group, or *phylum*.

Much greater diversity occurs among Invertebrates, which are grouped in eleven distinct phyla.

The *lowest Phylum* contains the *Protozoa*, which are microscopic, unicellular animals composed of a minute speck of protoplasm controlled by a nucleus. When a drop of pond-water is looked at under a microscope it is seen to contain numbers of minute organisms, many of which are moving rapidly in all directions. They are generally too small for details of form to be made out, but their vigorous movements show that they are certainly alive.

One of the largest of the unicellular animals is *Amœba* (Gr. *amoibē*, change). It lives in mud at the bottom of a pond and is just visible to the naked eye. It consists of a speck of greyish granular protoplasm of no definite shape, bordered by a colourless, non-granular peripheral portion. Embedded in the granular part is the dense nucleus, and there are also one or more *food-vacuoles* with ingested particles (p. 123). A large, hollow space which alternately appears and disappears is the *contractile vacuole* through which liquid waste is discharged. *Amœba* moves only by the flowing of the protoplasm (p. 147) and, in reproduction, one individual simply divides into two (p. 162).

Some *Protozoa* have protoplasmic threads, or flagella, by which movement is brought about, and some have a more complicated method of reproduction in which two individuals are concerned.

All the other animals in the world are made up of more than one cell. The simplest of these multicellular animals compose *Phylum II*, which includes *Hydra*, Jellyfish, Corals, and Sea Anemones. The special characteristics of the members of this phylum are that they have only one opening through which food is taken in and waste is got rid of, and they have no alimentary tract distinct from the body-cavity.

The Sponges which compose *Phylum III*, and the Starfishes and Sea Urchins of *Phylum IV* have a somewhat more complicated structure.

Phyla V to IX consist of worm-like forms. In all, as in the common Earthworm, the alimentary tract is distinct from the body-cavity. Their plan of structure can be represented by two cylinders, one enclosed within the other : the outer represents the body-wall; the inner stands for the alimentary canal; the space between the two represents the body-cavity (Fig. 73). The Earthworm has two apertures; one serves for the taking in of food, and through the other waste is expelled. The structural plan of all animals higher in the scale may be referred to this simple type.

The remaining two Invertebrate phyla, *Phyla X and XI*, are the groups of the Molluscs and the Arthropods.

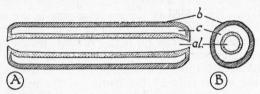

FIG. 73.—PLAN OF STRUCTURE OF EARTHWORM.

A, Longitudinal. B, Transverse. *al.*, alimentary tract; *b.*, body-wall; *c.*, cœlom.

The Molluscs, which include Snails, Mussels, and Limpets, have soft bodies protected in hard shells.

Arthropods (gr. *arthron*, a joint ; *podes*, feet) have *jointed* appendages, and their bodies and limbs are enclosed in a hard exoskeleton. To this phylum belong Insects, Spiders, and Crustaceans (Crab, Lobster, Shrimps, etc.).

The primary division of the Vegetable Kingdom is into the two groups of *Flowering* and *Non-flowering* Plants.

All Flowering Plants produce seeds. In these plants, as in Mammals, internal fertilization is followed by the retention of the fertilized egg. In its early development the embryo is protected and nourished by surrounding tissues of the parent. The mature seed contains, not only the young plant, but also all the food this needs in the early stages of its growth.

There are two classes of Flowering Plants. In the great majority the seeds are enclosed within a fruit. The cone-bearing trees, on the other hand, such as the Pine and Larch, bear seeds that are not enclosed in a fruit-case.

The Non-flowering Plants are grouped in four classes: Algæ, Fungi, Mosses and Liverworts, Ferns and Horsetails.

To the Algæ belong all the seaweeds and simple freshwater plants. Although they range in structure from unicellular forms such as *Chlamydomonas* to plants of some bulk like the Bladderwrack, none have the highly differentiated tissues of the higher plants. Generally speaking, Algæ live in water and take food and air from the surrounding water. Many seaweeds are brown and some of the most beautiful are red, but in all chlorophyll is present, the green colour being merely masked. When a branch of Bladderwrack is boiled in fresh water the brown colouring matter is dissolved and the branch becomes bright green. Both asexual and sexual methods of reproduction occur in different members of the class; in the latter case the egg is fertilized by motile spermatozoids.

Fungi are, for the most part, land plants. They include all Non-Flowering Plants that have no chlorophyll, and therefore live either as parasites or saprophytes. Yeast and Bacteria are unicellular forms; Moulds and Mildews are filamentous; large compact structures are characteristic of Mushrooms and Toadstools. But even the largest members of the class are very simple in structure; they have no true tissues like those of higher plants, but are made up of intertwining filaments. The Fungi are degenerate in the way in which they reproduce as well as in their method of nutrition—sexual reproduction tends to give place to asexual methods and, in the Toadstool families, reproduction depends entirely on asexual spores.

Mosses and Liverworts are also simple land plants, but of a distinctly higher grade than the Fungi. One individual moss plant is very small. The mossy " carpet " is formed by many plants living together, and their large communities cover wide areas on banks and in woods. Because their low growth prevents their being buffeted by the wind, and because they can withstand drought and cold, they often grow on high mountain slopes where vegetation is scarce. Mosses reproduce both sexually and asexually. In spring male and female sexual organs develop at the tips of the leafy shoots; in some Mosses both are borne by the same individual, in others they occur on different plants. Spermatozoids are set free and swim to the egg-cells. To this end the plant must, at this time, be in sufficiently damp surroundings for the journey to be accomplished. The fertilized egg develops *in situ* at the tip of the plant. It forms a long, thin " stalk " with a " fruit-body ", or capsule, at its apex. In the capsule dust-like spores are produced from which new moss plants arise.

The remaining group of Non-Flowering Plants is that of the Ferns and Horsetails. British Ferns are small plants, but in tropical countries Ferns grow to a considerable size. The tissues of Ferns are much more highly differentiated than those of Mosses : like Flowering Plants, they have a definite transport system for the conveyance of solutions from the soil and for the passage of elaborated food. They resemble Mosses in the way in which they reproduce. Asexual reproduction depends on spores, produced in spore-cases on the backs of fronds. When the spores germinate they do not give rise directly to the familiar Fern, but to flat, green, heart-shaped structures that are smaller than the nail of the little finger and produce the sexual organs. They may be seen on the earth of pots in which Ferns are growing in damp greenhouses. As in Mosses, spermatozoids reach the egg-cells by swimming. After fertilization a new Fern-plant develops from the fertilized egg.

All members of the Plant and Animal kingdoms live together in the world, whatever there may be of harmony or discord between them. All are struggling to get what they need for growth and development, and the success of one often depends upon the destruction of another. Certain animals feed on other animals, which in their turn get their nourishment from grass or other green plants, so that, broadly speaking, all animals are ultimately dependent upon the " grass of the field ". Such a " food chain " illustrates the inevitable interdependence of different forms of life.

That " no man liveth to himself " is only a limited truth. Actually " no living thing liveth to itself " in a world whose inhabitants, from the lowliest unicellular forms to the most complex animals and plants, are, at all times and in all places, in a state of interdependence.

When an individual dies its body disintegrates, and the elements of which it was composed are used once more, as they have been used over and over again in the past. The world owes its freedom from an accumulation of lifeless organisms to the unceasing work of Bacteria, which bring about disintegration. Thus in death, as in life, interrelations between individuals persist.

In Nature nothing is wasted. The history of every element may be traced through a cycle of changes until it returns again to its point of origin. All living things, both plant and animal, use up the oxygen of the air in respiration and give out carbon dioxide; the normal proportion of gases is restored by the photosynthesis of the green plant, which absorbs carbon dioxide and returns oxygen to the atmosphere (Fig. 74).

The carbon cycle is more complicated. The carbon dioxide of the atmosphere is used by the green plant in building up its food—carbohydrates, fats and proteins. Some of these elaborated materials are broken down immediately in the liberation of energy; some are

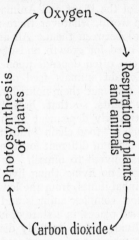

FIG. 74.—OXYGEN CYCLE.

stored for later use; some are used in the formation of the tissues of the plant. In time the tissues may be eaten by animals, or they may decay when the plant dies: in either case death, followed by decomposition brought about by bacterial action, gives back carbon dioxide to the atmosphere. The carbon cycle is shown in Fig. 75.

The nitrogen cycle is still more complex, but the element passes in the same way through a cycle of

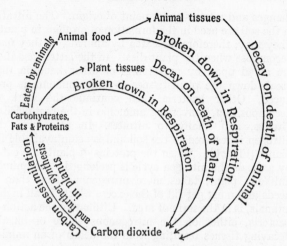

FIG. 75.—CARBON CYCLE.

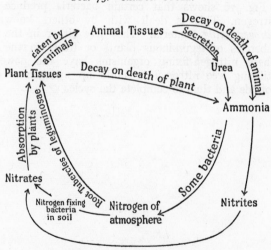

FIG. 76.—NITROGEN CYCLE.

changes and returns to its point of origin. The nitrates in the soil are used in the formation of proteins in plants. They may, therefore, be eaten by animals, or they may decompose when the plant dies. In the latter case they are acted upon by putrefying- or other bacteria that break down the plant-tissues so that ammonia is produced. Other bacteria then continue the work of decomposition, converting ammonia in the first place to nitrites, and finally to nitrates. In this form the nitrogen is restored to the soil and is again available for plants (Fig. 76). When the proteins of plants are eaten by animals the nitrogen cycle is prolonged. An animal, unlike a plant, takes more nitrogenous food than it needs and must get rid of the excess which, in all higher animals, is in the form of urea. Ultimately the action of bacteria, either on the nitrogenous waste or on the decaying tissues resulting from the death of an animal, restores nitrogen to the soil in the form of nitrates.

Fig. 76 shows that certain bacteria produce free nitrogen. This is dealt with by others known as *nitrogen-fixing* bacteria. They live either in the root tubercles of leguminous plants or freely in the soil. These nitrogen-fixing organisms have the power of utilizing free nitrogen to build up nitrogenous compounds and thus to complete the cycle.

SECTION IV
EVOLUTION AND HEREDITY

CHAPTER XVIII
EVOLUTION

PERHAPS to-day, more than ever before, the realization of an ever-changing world is forced upon us. The universe, both living and non-living, is always in a state of flux; to-day it is different from what it was yesterday, and to-morrow it will be different again. Nothing stands still. The face of the country, the pace of life, ideologies, and international relationships are all changing. Living things are born; reach maturity; give birth to other living things similar to, but not exactly like, themselves; and then they die. Nothing persists save change, for, paradoxically, change is the one thing that is permanent.

> ". . . you touch the nerve of change
> Then of life you have the clue.
> .   .   .   .
> Sameness locks no scurfy pond
> Here for Custom, crazy-fond;
> Change is on the wing to bud
> Rose in brain from rose in blood."

This constant change, which has been the rule since the world began, is responsible for the multitudinous forms of plant and animal life that exist to-day. Throughout the ages there has been " evolution ".

By " organic evolution " is meant, firstly, that the animals and plants which are living to-day are the direct descendants of those that have preceded them in time; secondly, that modifications in the descendants have occurred concurrently with changing surroundings; thirdly, that the modifications have been, on the whole, from the simpler to the more complex.

Abundant evidence that there has been such evolution is provided by the study of fossils. Geologists are able to compute the relative ages of different rock strata, and it is therefore possible to arrange, in time-series, the fossil remains of such animals and plants as have been found in the strata.

In Fig. 77 the forms of life that existed in successive geological epochs are indicated. The actual length of geological time cannot be ascertained. Estimates of the age of the oldest rocks have varied enormously. Some scientists have calculated it as 1,600 million; on the other hand it has been put as low as 25 million. There is also some divergence of view with respect to the classification of the successive strata into geological epochs, but the essential facts are well established: life began in the water and Invertebrate Animals lived before any Vertebrates appeared; Fishes preceded Amphibians; Amphibians were succeeded by Reptiles, which attained giant dimensions and were the dominant animals at one period of the world's history; the giant Reptiles in their turn became extinct; they were succeeded by Birds and Mammals, which are the dominant animals of our world to-day.

The record of the rocks reveals a similar story in the evolution of Plants, although the record in this case is much less complete; this is probably because there is not so much that can be preserved in plant-structure as in that of animals. Nevertheless the record shows clearly that the earliest Plants were simple in structure; that Non-Flowering Plants existed before Flowering Plants; that the earliest Flowering Plants were the Cone-bearing Trees; that these were dominant for a period and were later succeeded by the higher class of Flowering Plants—namely, those that form fruits in which seeds are enclosed.

Computed time in millions of years	Geological Epochs		Evolutionary history shown by fossil record
3	Quaternary, or Recent Tertiary, or Cainozoic		Age of mammals & birds & flowering plants
9	Secondary or Mesozoic	Cretaceous Jurassic Triassic	Giant reptiles and cone-bearing trees dominant
18	Primary or Palaeozoic	Permian	Rise of Reptiles
		Carboniferous	Age of giant amphibians & tree-ferns
		Devonian	Life on land established
		Silurian	Earliest land animals & plants
		Ordovician	First fishes, the earliest backboned animals
		Cambrian	Life abundant in sea.
30	Proterozoic Azoic		Life appeared

This table should be read from the bottom upwards

FIG. 77.—LIFE IN SUCCESSIVE GEOLOGICAL ERAS.

The fossil record does more than show the mere succession of life-forms in time. Sometimes it supplies a fossil link between two classes whose present-day representatives differ widely, and thus gives evidence of the derivation of one class from the other. A fossil has been found, for instance, which combines the charac-

FIG. 78.—RESTORATION OF ARCHÆOPTERYX (AFTER PYCRAFT).

The small figure is the skull.

teristics of modern Birds and Reptiles. The animal, to which the name *Archæopteryx* has been given, was bird-like; it had wings and feathers and was obviously a flying creature (Fig. 78). Its tail-feathers, however, were on either side of a long tail similar to that of a reptile. It had, too, a reptile's mouth, with teeth. Also, whereas the bones of the hand in the wing of a modern bird are very much reduced and are fused together, the thumb of the fossil bird is quite separate, as it is in reptiles. Only two of these fossils have been found; one of them is in the Natural History Museum at South Kensington.

There is yet a third way in which the rock record gives evidence of evolution; in adjacent beds fossils have been discovered of animals which differed slightly in successive epochs. The story of the evolution of the Horse is an excellent example of such a case. In the Tertiary beds of North America a connected series of fossils has been found, ranging from a small animal about the size of a hare, running on its toes, and having simple grinding-teeth, up to the high-stepping horse which has complicated grinding-teeth and stands on the tip-toe of the third digit only. During the time that this series of animals lived the physiographical conditions in North America were gradually changing from moist forest-land, with many streams, to meadows and prairies and a drier climate. Because food was more difficult to get, swifter movement was necessary, and efficient grinding-teeth were needed to crop the short grass of the dry prairies.

It is from fossils, then, that the main evidence for evolution is obtained. But there are other subsidiary lines of evidence all of which, taken together, leave no doubt as to its truth.

The geographical distribution of many living things is explicable only on the theory of evolution. The tortoises of the Galapagos Islands are an illustration of this point. When Charles Darwin visited these islands in 1831 he studied the variations in the Giant Tortoises that inhabited them. He found that each island had its own particular species of tortoise, which was slightly different both from that of any other island, and from the Giant Tortoise of the mainland. He also found that the island tortoises differed less from each other than from the species on the mainland. Geological evidence supports the conclusion that the Galapagos Islands were originally part of the mainland of South America; from it the island-mass became separated and, at a much later period of time, split up into separate islands. This being so, the present distribution of tortoises can be explained on the evolutionary hypothesis that modifications in descendants accompany change in conditions. The degree of modification would tend to be proportional to the lapse of time, and the tortoises on the several islands would therefore differ less from one another than from the Giant Tortoise of the mainland. Darwin was deeply impressed by this geographical distribution, and wrote that he felt himself " brought near to the very act of creation ".

The theory of evolution is also strengthened by the similarities in the development of all living things. It has been said that in its development every animal climbs up its own genealogical tree. In a great measure this is true. All animals and plants begin life as a single cell. If the first forms of life were unicellular, then every present-day living thing, in its initial stage, harks back to its original ancestor. In the development of the Frog subsequent steps of the " climb " are clear : from the fertilized egg-cell a tadpole develops which has, for a time, external gills ; when these are replaced by internal gills the tadpole breathes like a fish ; finally lungs develop, and the Frog leaves the water for the land.

The early embryological development of all multi-cellular animals is similar. Even in the later stages of pre-natal development there is remarkable similarity in the embryological structure of individuals that differ widely one from another when they are born.

The uniformity in the skeletal structure of Vertebrates is strong evidence of their descent from a common ancestor. Although the limbs of back-boned animals are used for different purposes, they are all built on the same general plan. Darwin writes : " How inexplicable is the similar pattern of the hand of a man, the foot of a dog, the wing of a bat, the flipper of a seal, on the doctrine of independent acts of creation.''

There are structures in the human body that seem utterly meaningless until their evolutionary history is known. The appendix, for instance, is apparently not only useless to Man, but is actually often harmful, and its presence in human beings only becomes intelligible when its work in the lower Mammals is understood. It then appears that the appendix in Man is something without value that he has inherited; something '' left over '', as it were—a *vestige* of an organ that played a useful part in the physiological processes of his ancestors. There are many such vestigial organs. In the inner corner of our eye is a vestige of a third eyelid; such an eyelid is functional in Birds and Rabbits. Hairs on various parts of the human body are reminiscent of the hairy covering of our ancestors. Our external ear, that no longer functions as a receiver of sound, is an interesting, but useless, heirloom.

There is, then, definite and weighty evidence to show that evolution has taken place and is still continuing. The *fact* of evolution seems to be well established, but the consideration of *how* it has come about introduces difficult problems. Many theories have been put forward in explanation of the evolution of the organic world, but, as yet, no real solution has been found.

The necessary factors are *variation* and *heredity*. There could be no evolution if all offspring were exactly like their parents; evolution would be equally impossible if such variations as do occur could not be handed on to the next generation.

The following questions then arise : How do changes occur? and, How is the equipment of the parent passed on to the offspring?

Opinion as to the origin of variations is still divided. Darwin wrote : '' Our ignorance of the laws of variation is profound.'' The most one can say to-day is that this ignorance is now, perhaps, a little less profound. As far as work on heredity is concerned—that is, on the " passing on "—definite progress has been made.

It is erroneous to think that the idea of evolution originated with Darwin. Aristotle discussed it in his far-away day. What Charles Darwin did was to formulate a theory, backed by such wealth of observation that it became practically impossible to think of Biology except in evolutionary terms.

Modern theories relating to organic evolution begin with the work of Lamarck (1744–1829). Lamarck put forward a doctrine which is known as the *Transmission of Acquired Characters* and which, during the past hundred years, has perhaps been more discussed than any other scientific theory.

By an " acquired character " is meant one that an individual has come by during his lifetime, as distinct from one that he has inherited from his parents.

Briefly stated the theory of the transmission of acquired characters maintains that any modifications acquired by individuals, either because of the use or disuse of parts, or because of some change in environment, may be transmitted to their offspring. On this hypothesis the long neck of Giraffes results from their stretching upwards, in one generation after another, for the most tender leaves at the tips of the branches of the trees on which they feed; Snakes have become long and flexible, and have lost their useless limbs as a result, generation after generation, of stretching forward and gliding through the undergrowth which is their home; wading-birds of the present day have long legs and webbed feet because the waders of the past stretched their legs so that they might venture further out into the water, and spread their toes to keep themselves from sinking.

It is a matter of common observation and experience that structures are strengthened by use and tend to degenerate with disuse. At the outset, therefore,

Lamarck's theory seems to provide a good working hypothesis. Further, one would like to think that the good that is acquired in one generation can be transmitted to the next. But, during the period of time that separates Lamarck's day from ours, there has been no conclusive experimental evidence to prove that acquired characters are transmitted. Nevertheless the theory that such characters cannot in any way be transmitted should not hastily be ruled out. It may be that in some way not yet understood these may be passed on from one generation to the next.

The characters of any organism are of two distinct kinds : *adaptive* characters are those that show relationship between an organism and its surroundings, and *diagnostic* characters are those that have no such relationship. It may be that evolution cannot be explained by one universal formula, but that Lamarck's theory, in some modified form, may be true of adaptive characters. Very many experiments have been carried out in an attempt to prove this possibility. An account of one such experiment is very instructive : Macdougall put rats into a tank which they could leave only by swimming. He gave them two landing-places. One of these was lighted, the other was dark. When landing on the lighted landing the rat received an electric shock. The position of the landing-places was continually changed. In the first few generations it took more than a hundred trials before the rats learned that they could avoid the electric shock by leaving the water from the dark landing. The number of trials gradually decreased until, in the twenty-third generation, the rats made only twenty-five trials before they learned how to avoid the shock.

The theory put forward by Darwin in his " Origin of Species ", published in 1859, is the *Theory of Natural Selection*. Natural selection has been aptly described by Sir Arthur Thompson as " nature's sifting ", for it is essentially a sifting process in which the weakest goes to the wall.

The basis of the theory is that the offspring of any parents are neither exactly like their parents nor each other. Darwin did not attempt to explain this tendency to vary; he accepted it as a primary fact of life. Offspring are born into an overcrowded world, consequently there is a " *struggle for existence* "—there is competition for necessary food, light, and air. As the individuals are not exactly alike, it will come about that any variation that gives a slight advantage to its possessor may help him to live at the expense of the less fortunate—that is, there will be " *survival of the fittest* ".

An illustration that was used to explain Lamarck's view of the transmission of acquired characters applies equally as an example of natural selection. The lengths of the necks of all the Giraffes of any generation will not be identical; the animals that have slightly longer necks than their fellows will get the best food and will thus tend to survive; they will, therefore, pass on their advantageous equipment to their offspring.

Acceptance of Darwin's theory of evolution depends on the verification of its two hypotheses : (*a*) that the minute, fluctuating variations inherent in living things are the basis on which evolution works : (*b*) that natural selection takes place.

This latter point, the fact of natural selection, is a matter of easy verification. A striking experiment, which is now classical, was made by the Italian naturalist, Cesnola. In Italy there are two varieties of the Praying Mantis; one is green and feeds on grass; the other is brown and its food is withered foliage. Cesnola tethered twenty-three of the green insects on grass, and twenty brown ones on withered leaves. All were alive at the end of seventeen days. He then tethered twenty-five green insects on brown grass and in eleven days' time they were all dead. After a period of seventeen days, only

ten were alive out of forty-five brown ones tethered on
green grass. In all cases the deaths were due to the
attacks of birds and ants, and not to the change of food.
This experiment shows clearly the survival value of
protective colour.

That individuals tend to vary, and that natural selection takes place, is beyond argument. It does not,
however, follow that Darwin's view of evolution as
determined by the piling up, generation after generation,
of " minute variations or fluctuations " is the correct one.
Indeed, common observations seem to point the other
way.   The children of tall parents, for instance, tend to
be above the average height, but generally speaking are
not taller than their parents.   The tendency in later
generations is to return to the mean of the species.

There are other difficulties in the way of the acceptance
of the Darwinian theory.

To have survival value a variation would have to be
advantageous at every step; but many modifications
occur in which this is not the case.   The lips of the
corolla of the Snapdragon (*Antirrhinum*) are so tightly
closed that only a Bumble-bee can force an entrance and
bring about pollination.   Such a modification could
hardly have arisen by the piling up of minute variations,
because no benefit would result until the petals met so
firmly that other insects were kept out.

Then, again, often in evolutionary change many
different structures are affected.   To have survival value
all these structures would have to vary simultaneously
in a corresponding direction.   In the case of the evolution of the Horse (p. 187) it would be necessary to assume,
on the Darwinian hypothesis, that changes occurred
simultaneously, and in a corresponding direction, in the
bones and muscles of the leg, the uplift of the heel, the
elongation of the third digit, and in the marked development of the grinding surfaces of the teeth.   Moreover,
such variations would have had to go on occurring

G

simultaneously for an indefinite period of time. It seems well-nigh impossible that all these assumptions could be true.

Again, one would expect to find many links between different species; but this is not so: species are clearly cut and sharply defined.

Yet another difficulty in the way of acceptance of Darwin's hypothesis is that it offers no explanation of the persistence of useless structures, which could hardly persist in a world entirely regulated by the survival of the fittest.

The variations on which Darwin based his hypothesis were small and occurred in all directions. They were "continuous variations, or fluctuations". At the same time he recognized the occurrence of greater variations with no intermediate forms. To such "discontinuous variations" which he termed "sports" he did not assign much significance. The importance of such "sports". or "mutations", is considered later (p. 196).

One outstanding result of Darwin's work was that he set all the world thinking. He had put forward a clear, working hypothesis, backed by a wealth of observation and experiment, to account for existing living forms. His work was an incentive to Biological research, not only on the vexed question of the origin of species, but also on the whole question of heredity. The problems eagerly debated were : How do variations occur? Are acquired characters transmitted? Are little variations or fluctuations passed on, or do the descendants tend to return to the mean?

With regard to Lamarck's contention that acquired characters are transmitted, Darwin considered that under certain circumstances this might occur, but he ruled out the possibility of their transmission being the basis of evolution. To Darwin evolution was due to variations that are inherent—that is, born in the individual—and not to those that are acquired during his lifetime.

The first serious opponent of Lamarck was Weismann. His work, published in 1892, was based entirely on the intimate *cell-structure* of organisms and was greatly helped by the improvement in microscopes and microscopic technique. Weismann's theory may be briefly summarized as follows : a new individual develops from a fertilized egg, produced by the fusion of two germ-cells (the gametes) ; the whole of the inheritance of any individual must, therefore, be contained in the fertilized egg ; when this divides to form the embryo some of the cells thus produced form the *body* of the organism and therefore come to an end with the death of the body ; other cells give rise to *germ-cells*, which carry over to the next generation ; there is thus continuity of germinal protoplasm from one generation to another ; it is, consequently, the germ-cells, and the germ-cells only, that are responsible for passing on the inheritance. Following this reasoning to its logical conclusion, Weismann contended that what happens in the *body* of the individual cannot possibly affect the offspring—that is, no *acquired* character can be passed on.

When Weismann wrote in 1892, the reduction division of the nucleus (meiosis, p. 121) had not been seen. Nevertheless he prophesied that, at some time during the life-history of every animal and plant, the number of chromosomes of certain cells must be reduced to half ; that the gametes ultimately produced from these cells would then contain only half the number of chromosomes characteristic of the species ; and that, on the fusion of the nuclei in fertilization, the original number would be restored. That such reduction actually occurs was soon proved to be the case. The fulfilment of his prophesy added greatly to the number of Weismann's adherents and Lamarck's theory received a set-back.

In the light of still further research neither Lamarck's

theory of " use ", nor Darwin's of " minute continuous fluctuations ", seemed adequate as an explanation of the cause of evolutionary change.

In 1901 Hugo de Vries published his *Mutation Theory*. He claimed that " sports ", which Darwin had considered of little significance, were all-important, and contended that evolution depended, not upon the piling-up of continuous small fluctuations, but upon discontinuous variations, or *mutations*.

De Vries based his theory on his work on a species of Evening Primrose (*Oenothera Lamarckiana*), that he found growing wild in a potato field at Hilversum, and in a state of " mutation ". The number of new types or " sports " produced from the one species as a result of mutation was considerable, and de Vries found that many of them bred true.

His mutation theory, then, asserts that new species arise suddenly. Such a theory would account for the non-existence of intermediate forms, and also for the survival of useless variations.

Familiar cases of mutation are the Copper Beech and the Shirley Poppy. The former first appeared in the seventeenth century, and has bred true ever since. The latter was the discovery, in 1880, of the Vicar of Shirley ; in his garden he sowed the seeds of the one plant he had found, and thus ensured the preservation of the " sports ".

Whether the variations which determine evolution are minute continuous fluctuations as Darwin believed, or whether they are sudden and discontinuous as contended by de Vries, the causes of the variations are as yet imperfectly understood. The way in which an entirely new character arises in any species is still unsolved ; the elucidation may be the work of the Biologists of the future.

CHAPTER XIX

HEREDITY

FROM the time of the publication of the " Origin of Species " in 1859 until the end of the nineteenth century, attempts to solve the problems of evolution followed the line of discussion and controversy rather than of research.

Since the beginning of this century a different outlook has prevailed. It has been realized that it was, perhaps, premature to seek the causes of variations until much more was known as to their method of operating.

Three different ways of investigating variation and inheritance have been followed : experimental breeding ; the microscopic study of the germ-cells ; the compiling of statistics.

Modern breeding experiments begin with the work of an Austrian monk, Gregor Mendel (1822–1884). The scientific world of his time was busy with arguments and debates, and it was not until his work was rediscovered in the early days of this century that its significance was understood.

With the aim of fixing certain particular characters many experiments in breeding had, of course, been carried on before Mendel. By the rough-and-ready method of mating individuals whose characters approached most nearly to those desired, fairly satisfactory results were obtained in the offspring. Mendel's work, unlike that of his predecessors, was definitely selective— he focused attention on *one* character at *one* time. His earlier experiments were on the Garden Pea, which is self-fertilized, and of which there are several distinct varieties: some plants have *round*, others *wrinkled* seeds; some have *yellow*, others *green* seeds; some plants are *tall*, others are *dwarf*. Mendel produced his hybrids by cross-pollinating varieties that showed one of these pairs of characters; from the seeds of the hybrid thus obtained he grew several further, self-fertilized generations.

The stigmas of flowers of a tall plant were brushed with pollen from the stamens of flowers of a dwarf plant. Actually it made no difference which way the cross was effected; the results were just the same when pollen from a tall plant was brushed over the stigmas of the flowers of a dwarf.

From the seeds produced as a result of the cross-pollination hybrid plants were grown. These were not midway in height between the tall and dwarf parents, as might have been expected. They were all tall. This hybrid generation is now always referred to as the F_1 (first filial) generation.

The tall hybrid plants were left to themselves and, therefore, they were self-fertilized. From their seeds another generation was grown (the F_2 generation) in which some plants were tall and some were dwarf, the proportion being three tall to one dwarf. As the dwarf character now reappeared, it could not have been entirely lost in the F_1 generation, but was, in that generation, masked by the character of tallness. Mendel gave the terms *Dominant* and *Recessive* to the characters of " tallness " and " dwarfness " respectively.

Seeds from dwarf plants of the F_2 generation produced dwarf plants *only*, and continued to do so for as many generations as the experiments were carried on.

The seeds from the tall plants on the other hand did not all behave alike: one-third of these seeds bred true, producing tall plants only; the other two-thirds behaved like the original hybrid, giving rise to tall and dwarf plants in the proportion of three to one.

The following table shows the results obtained :—

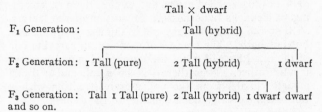

F₁ Generation : Tall (hybrid)

F₂ Generation : 1 Tall (pure)   2 Tall (hybrid)   1 dwarf

F₃ Generation :   Tall 1 Tall (pure) 2 Tall (hybrid) 1 dwarf dwarf
and so on.

On experimenting with plants whose seeds showed the characters of roundness and wrinkledness, and of yellowness and greenness, Mendel obtained similar results. He found that the quality of roundness was dominant to that of wrinkledness, and yellow was dominant to green.

From his experiments Mendel deduced that characters were transmitted from parent to offspring separately and independently of each other. These separate characters he called *unit factors*; in modern genetic language they are now called *genes*. The total inheritance of any individual is, according to Mendel, *the sum of the inherited unit factors*. He further stated that these unit factors might be arranged in pairs. Such pairs of contrasting unit factors are now called *allelomorphs*.

In order to account for the numerical results of his experiments, Mendel concluded that no gamete could carry both factors of an allelomorphic pair. The gamete, for instance, may carry the quality of tallness *or* dwarfness, but it cannot carry both; it may carry the character of roundness *or* wrinkledness, but never both. This important deduction is now known as the law of the *Purity of the Gamete* : purity, that is, with respect to one factor of an allelomorphic pair.

When the original cross is effected, a gamete carrying the quality for tallness unites with a gamete carrying the quality for dwarfness. All the cells of the hybrid pea plant (F₁), that results from this act of fertilization, must contain both factors. When, however, the cells divide to form pollen grains and ovules, there is, according to Mendel's hypothesis, a separation of the factors, so that the gametes carry *either* tallness *or* dwarfness, but not both. The number of gametes (n) carrying one of the qualities will equal the number of gametes carrying the other. Thus there will be n tall and n dwarf gametes (male) from the pollen-grains, uniting with n tall and n dwarf gametes (female) in the ovules.

When self-pollination takes place, a male gamete bearing the factor for tallness may find its way to an ovule whose egg carries the quality *either* of tallness *or* of dwarfness : the chances are equal. Similarly, male gametes with the factor for dwarfness have an equal chance of fertilizing ovules carrying tallness or dwarfness. Therefore the seeds resulting from these acts of fertilization may carry both characters, or a double dose of one; and the F_2 generation of plants will be tall–tall, tall–dwarf, dwarf–tall, dwarf–dwarf, in equal numbers. That is, a quarter will be pure tall, a quarter pure dwarf, and a half hybrid. But, as tallness is the dominant character, all the hybrid plants grow tall, like the pure tall, so that the F_2 generation is in the proportion of three tall plants to one dwarf—this is the numerical result that was obtained by Mendel, and thus proves his hypothesis.

A simple experiment illustrates the numerical result that follows the haphazard fusion of gametes. Beads are used to represent the male gametes, 100 being red and 100 green. These are put into a basin A, and are thoroughly mixed. The female gametes are represented in the same way, and 100 red beads and 100 green are put into a second basin, B. Basin A, then, represents the male parent, and basin B the female. A bead is then taken at random from each basin and the pair placed on the table. This pair represents the plant, or *zygote*, produced by the coupling of qualities, or unit factors, in this case " redness " and " blueness ". When all the pairs, thus picked quite at haphazard, are on the table, their number is found to approximate to 100 red-blue, 50 red–red, and 50 blue–red. Each pair contains either both factors of an allelomorphic pair or two doses of one factor. The terms *heterozygote* (Greek *heteros*, different) and *homozygote* (Greek *homos*, same) are used to distinguish the hybrid from the pure individual with reference to any unit factor. It may be simpler to carry out this experiment with 400 dried peas, 200 of which are dyed by putting them into red ink, and 200 of which are left uncoloured.

Since the re-discovery of Mendel's records in 1900, a vast amount of experimental work has been carried out on similar lines to his, giving widespread confirmation of his theories of inheritance both in animals and plants. One interesting example of " Mendelian inheritance " is the colour of the human eye; here brown is dominant to blue, therefore two blue-eyed parents cannot have a brown-eyed child.

In carrying out experimental work on Mendelian lines, however, difficulties were encountered. It was realized that inheritance was not so straightforward as the earlier experiments of Mendel seemed to indicate.

It was soon apparent that dominance was not universal, for the hybrid does not, in all cases, show a dominant character. The " theory of dominance " has, therefore, been replaced by the *Presence and Absence Theory*. According to this theory an allelomorphic " pair " consists of the presence of a certain quality and its absence. In the case of roundness and wrinkledness, for instance, one gamete may carry " roundness " and the other " absence of roundness ". Thus the factor " roundness " may be " present ", or it may be " absent ". If it is absent from both gametes the recessive quality of " wrinkledness " characterizes the offspring.

Other difficulties that have arisen can be explained along Mendelian lines.

Knowledge of the laws of Mendelian inheritance is of great practical value, as is shown, for example, in the research work carried out on Wheat. There is a quality in Wheat known as " strength " which is essential for producing flour that will make a good loaf. This quality was lacking in English wheat, and therefore grain had to be imported from America and Canada. British wheats had the further disadvantage that they were all liable to attacks of " rust ". Professor Biffen of Cambridge proved that many characteristics of Wheat behave as simple Mendelian allelomorphs. By suitable crossing of British with American varieties he has succeeded in raising a Wheat which yields a good crop, makes acceptable bread, and is immune from rust.

Mendelian laws are deduced entirely from experiments on hybridization, whereby existing characters are re-grouped and thus give variety in the offspring. But hybridization could originate new characters only in so far as the re-grouping could produce something entirely new. Recent experiments have tended to show that this may be the case and, if these results are confirmed, they would have great evolutionary significance. But hybridization could not be the sole basis of evolution, for mutations often occur in its absence. As the experiments of de Vries (p. 196) were made on one species only of the Evening Primrose, hybridization played no part in the results.

The microscopic study of germ-cells is a second method of investigating the laws of inheritance. In recent years much evidence has been brought forward proving that there is connection between chromosomes and hereditary characters. Assuming that each chromosome is a bearer of a portion of the inheritance, and that it is not the same at all parts of its length, it follows that its lengthwise split in nuclear division ensures that all the characters carried by the original chromosome pass equally to each daughter-cell.

In fertilization, apart from the sex-chromosome which is considered later (p. 205), each gamete carries the same number of chromosomes, X. Therefore the fertilized egg has 2X chromosomes. In the development of the embryo from the fertilized egg, 2X chromosomes are formed at each cell division; of these, X are derived from the male parent and X from the female. Such cell-division continues throughout the greater part of the life of the individual. Preceding the formation of gametes, however, there is a difference in the behaviour of chromosomes at one cell-division : in the division of cells from which gametes will ultimately be produced the chromosomes do not split lengthwise, but remain undivided, and half their number form the nucleus of each daughter-cell (p. 121).

In the early stage (*synapsis*) of this " reduction division " the chromosomes arrange themselves in a number of close pairs (Fig. 48). Subsequently one member, and one member *only*, of each pair, takes part in the formation of each daughter-nucleus. It appears, therefore, as if this close-pairing of chromosomes in synapsis was for the purpose of getting certain characteristics distributed to the resulting gametes.

In many cases chromosomes differ obviously in size and shape and are, therefore, readily identified. In synapsis it is seen that their " pairing " is not haphazard, but takes place between chromosomes of corresponding shape and size. Furthermore it has been established that these pairs of chromosomes, identifiable by their peculiarities, are present in every cell of the body, including its initial cell—the fertilized egg. It must be presumed, therefore, that of the two sets of chromosomes present in the fertilized egg, one set has been contributed by the male gamete, and the other by the female. Evidently, then, " pairing " at synapsis occurs between chromosomes one of which bears the male inheritance, and the other a corresponding set of qualities from the female parent.

As an example the qualities of roundness and wrinkledness in peas may be considered. The plant may be supposed to have inherited roundness from the male parent by way of the pollen-grain, and wrinkledness from the female by way of the ovule. In the ordinary nuclear divisions of the plant the factors for roundness and wrinkledness will be uniformly distributed, because each chromosome splits down its entire length. But preceding the formation of gametes—that is in the synapsis stage of the reduction division—there will be a chromosome-pair that carries the factor for roundness in one member and the quality for wrinkledness in the other. When the nucleus divides and the paired chromosomes separate, " roundness " will be carried to one daughter-nucleus, and " wrinkledness " to the other. It is impossible for both " roundness " and " wrinkledness " to be present in the same daughter-cell. As it is the division of these daughter-cells that ultimately produces the gametes, it follows that no gamete can contain factors both for roundness and wrinkledness—that is, no gamete can carry both factors of an allelomorphic pair. Mendel's law of " the purity of the gamete " thus receives confirmation from the evidence of *cytology*, the study of nuclear behaviour.

There would be an impossible " cumbering " of chromosomes if each carried only one allelomorphic pair of qualities. Numbers of characteristics must necessarily be carried by the same chromosome. That such " linkage " of characters does occur has been worked out most exhaustively by Professor T. H. Morgan, in the Banana Fly. In this fly he has established, for instance, that the factors for grey body and long wings, and also those for black body and vestigial wings, are always linked together and cannot be transmitted separately to the offspring.

If all the characters carried by a chromosome were united in one linkage group only, the number of possible variations in the offspring would be small, because the number of chromosomes is never great. It is therefore assumed that in each chromosome there are several linkage groups.

De Vries suggested that there might be an interchange of a group of allelomorphic characters between a pair of chromosomes during synapsis, so that the separating chromosomes are not exactly the same as those that approached one another. In support of this view Professor Morgan and other investigators have established the fact that sometimes, during synapsis, the chromosomes twist on one another and a break occurs at the twist, so that what was part of one chromosome becomes part of another. Such " cross-overs " would give infinite possibilities of variation in offspring, without affecting the purity of the gamete with respect to any factor of an allelomorphic pair.

Up to the beginning of this century the determination of sex was thought to be a question of environment, probably influenced largely by the nutrition of the developing embryo. It has now, in a large number of cases, been proved to depend on the presence or absence of an odd, unpaired chromosome, so that the sex of any organism is already fixed in the fertilized egg. Support for this conclusion is given in " identical twins " which develop from *one* fertilized egg and are always of the same sex.

The presence of an unpaired chromosome has been determined in the nuclei of the males of many species. It is known as the " sex-chromosome ", or *idiochromosome*. In the nuclei of the female of the species there are two idiochromosomes which pair in the normal way during the synapsis stage of the reduction division.

But in the synapsis stage of the reduction division of the male the single idiochromosome has nothing to pair with; therefore, when the nucleus divides, the sex-chromosome passes into one of the daughter-cells and the other is left without any corresponding chromosome. It follows, from this, that two kinds of male gametes are produced, because one is short of a chromosome. All the female gametes have an equal number of chromosomes, therefore when fertilization occurs two kinds of fertilized eggs must be produced in equal numbers : half of them will have *two* idiochromosomes and will therefore produce female individuals; the other half, with only *one* idiochromosome, will develop into males.

Sex-limited transmission—that is, the transmission of certain characters by one sex only—is capable of simple explanation if it is assumed that such characters are carried by the idiochromosomes. Colour-blindness, which is fairly common among males, is an illustration of sex-limited transmission.

The term *biometry* is applied to the statistical method of studying the laws of variation and heredity. The method consists essentially in counting or measuring, in a large number of individuals, definite characters which are capable of exact measurement. In this way the amount and the character of normal variation can be determined. That variations do occur between individuals, or parts of individuals, of the same species is a matter of simple observation. It is the work of the biometrician to measure these variations, to determine their occurrence, and to try to discover their effect on inheritance—that is, to find out whether the " minute continuous fluctuations " of Darwin can determine evolution. The following statistics given by Ward Cutler are an example of such work : The heights of 8585 men were found to vary continuously between 55 and 77 inches; the greatest number were between 67 and 69 inches; there was a gradual decrease in numbers as the heights differed more and more from this.

Such variations are of common occurrence, and it is interesting to plot curves of simple instances.

From a number of statistics it has been worked out that there is a definite degree of likeness between the characters of parents and their offspring. If the average height of a large number of men is known, then the average height of their offspring can be calculated. The degree of resemblance is greater when both parents are taken into account, and greater still when grandparents also are considered.

From the various data obtained by such methods the *Law of Ancestral Inheritance* was deduced. Sir Francis Galton concluded that parents contributed one half the inheritance, grandparents one quarter, great-grandparents one eighth, and so on. These figures were modified by Professor Karl Pearson, who estimated that the parents contributed more than half the inheritance and that the series diminished more rapidly.

It must be remembered that the methods of biometry are purely statistical and *their results are averages*. The law of ancestral inheritance cannot hold good for isolated cases : Mendelian experiments prove that, as far as certain qualities are concerned, some ancestors contribute nothing at all. Nevertheless the law holds when large numbers are under consideration.

Biometrical calculations depend largely on advanced mathematics, therefore the way in which biometry affects the Darwinian outlook can only be simply summarized here.

The question is : Can selection alter the normal course of variation? Is it possible, for instance, to breed a race of taller men? Superficial observation goes to show that the offspring of tall human parents are above the average height, but not taller than their parents, the tendency being to return to the mean.

How far, then, can a race be altered by selective breeding?

It is the custom for breeders to cross individuals that have the particular quality desired. Karl Pearson, assuming the law of ancestral inheritance, has calculated that the " selection value " of such a cross is very great for the first few generations, rising to as much as 90 per cent. of the selected quality; but after that further selection has very little effect. If this is so, and if the selection value never rises above 100 per cent., then evolution is not the result of selection.

The important work of Professor Johannsen and other investigators seems to confirm this conclusion. Johannsen chose Beans and Barley for his experiments, because these plants are self-fertilized. The character selected was the weight of the seed. The normal curve for the bean-population as a whole was first plotted. Then Johannsen plotted the seed-weight of plants all produced from a single parent. He called this a *Pure Line*. Its curve differed from that of the general bean-population. On testing other pure lines he found that each had its own special curve.

Individuals from pure lines which differed widely from the normal curve were then selected for experiment, and the important result was obtained that the offspring of such individuals regressed to the curve of their own pure line.

The conclusion was thus reached that selection within a pure line produces no effect. If this is so, then the gradual petering out of the effect of selection is explained : selection consists in the partial separation of those lines which have, in a marked degree, the quality that is desired, because the breeder retains the individuals that have this particular quality and discards the rest; therefore each generation that he breeds approaches more and more nearly to a pure line.

On this theory the particular character of any individual has no influence on descendants; what matters is the type of pure line to which he belongs.

The present position of our knowledge on this difficult question of evolution and heredity can now be briefly summarized.

It has been shown that evolution depends on variation and heredity, and that variation in an individual may be inherent or may be acquired during his lifetime.

It is clear that natural selection is at all times operative, weeding out individuals whose variations make them less fit to survive in the struggle for existence. But natural selection by itself can only act on variations that exist; it cannot produce anything new.

The great problem that still awaits solution is that of the origin of transmittable variations.

That modifications can be acquired is apparent, but there is no direct experimental evidence to show that such characters are transmitted.

An acquired character produced by use, either as a response to some demand of the environment or to the urge of the individual, is something new as far as that individual is concerned. If such an acquired character could, even in the minutest degree, be passed on to the next generation, the ultimate cumulative effect would be that the acquired character had become a habit. The hypothesis of the transmission of acquired characters gives a motive and reason for evolution which all the other theories lack. According to this theory " habit is the driving force of evolution ". Proof of the theory would alter our whole conception of the relative importance of " nature " and " nurture ", and would have the greatest possible influence on all social questions. The absence of any experimental proof that such transmission does take place may be due to the long stretch of time that is necessary for cumulative causes to result in a fixed habit.

It is conceivable that, in some way, the germ-cells may be influenced by what happens in the body. There is no absolute shutting-off of one cell from another. Even in plants there is protoplasmic connection between living cells through their walls. The possibility that cells do influence one another cannot be ruled out. The importance of the influence of glandular secretions (hormones) is only just beginning to be recognized. If, in some way, the germ-cells are affected by the body-cells, then what happens during the life of an individual may influence his germ-plasm and, ultimately, his offspring. In some such modified form there may be a broad basis of truth in the theory of Lamarck.

Apparently evolution does not depend on germinal continuous variations, because offspring tend to regress, and the effect of selective breeding dies out after a certain number of generations.

Discontinuous variations, on the other hand, do produce new variations which breed true. Mutations, whether produced by hybridization or not, are caused by the " shufflings " of the factors carried in the separate chromosomes. It has been seen that the number of different groupings may be increased indefinitely by " linkage " and " crossing-over ". But whether this fresh combination of *existing* factors can result in the origin of *new* ones still awaits confirmation. Yet, again and again, something new must have been introduced into the inheritance, if all the higher forms of life that exist to-day had their origin in some such lowly ancestor as *Amœba*.

" Some are born great, some achieve greatness, some have greatness thrust upon them." As far as the *individual* is concerned, it is good to achieve greatness or to have it thrust upon one ; such greatness is an acquired character. As far as the *race* is concerned it is all-important to be born great, because this greatness is inherent.

Eugenics, which Galton has defined as " the science of being well-born ", is the application of the principles of heredity to Man. As it is established, beyond question, that some of the germinal inheritance of the parent is passed on to the offspring, to be " well-born " is a most important attribute.

Knowledge of human heredity must necessarily be obtained mainly by statistical methods, and enlightening records have been kept of various families. A classic example is that of the Jukes family. The original Jukes was an intemperate waster from the American backwoods; out of more than 1000 of his descendants the histories of 540 are known with very fair accuracy, and most of the others are known in part. About one third died in infancy; 310 were paupers; 440 were physical wrecks; 130 were convicted criminals, 7 of whom were murderers; all evaded school education; only 20 learned a trade and, of these, 10 learned it perforce, in State prisons !

In contrast to this family are the 1394 descendants of Jonathan Edwards, the American divine. These included professors, doctors, writers, judges, and politicians. Not one of the 1394 was ever known to commit a crime !

Galton collected information relating to 80 cases of supposed identical twins. He found that in all cases they closely resembled one another in character and disposition, even when they were brought up under dissimilar conditions.

More recently interest was focused on a family of " quins ". As far as is known, no quintuplets were ever before reared. The " quins " were identical " twins ". Physically they had many points of resemblance : they were all of the same sex; they all belonged to the same blood-group; all had a slight webfootedness between the second and third toes. In this case the theory was that the fertilized egg divided twice, forming four separate cells, and that one of these divided again. Thus three of the quins were the result of the second division of the egg, and two of its third division. This would account for the fact that two of the children were smaller and more retarded in development than the other three; compared with the others both were long-sighted; both had a trace of cross-eyes; both grasped objects in a different way from the other three. Although the children were under the same environmental conditions as far as it was possible to make them, yet, as they grew older, they showed distinct personalities.

Many human characteristics have been shown to be hereditary : artistic ability and a cheerful disposition, for instance; and such defects as deafness, colour-blindness, hæmophilia, and insanity. It is difficult to get more than scattered data, but such defects as those quoted seem definitely due to the lack of some factor in the germ-plasm. If this be so, the occurrence of the defect in some only of the offspring would be accounted for. In a record taken in America 25·9 per cent. of the offspring of two deaf parents were deaf. Probably both parents had inherited deafness from one of their parents, and the deafness probably depended upon a certain grouping of factors in the chromosomes. The deafness of the offspring would then depend on the presence of this particular linkage-group in the uniting gametes to which they owed their being. If this is so, if any defect, such as deafness, in the offspring, depends on the combination of the correct factors for the particular defect, it is important to realize that such a combination is more likely to happen when both parents come, either from the same, or from a nearly related, strain. For this reason it is unwise for marriages to take place between those who are nearly akin.

In the past natural selection has, to a great extent, weeded out the unfit so that the " well-born " have had a chance to survive and breed. In a state of human civilization Natural Selection is no longer operative and the question arises : What is to be substituted for it?

Not only must the improvement of the individual be considered, but also the improvement of the race. Education, mental and physical, and all social services are concerned with the former. This is natural, because existing conditions are those of which we are always conscious. It is, however, of the greatest importance that, while the betterment of the individual is not neglected, the duty to the race that is to come should be remembered. As Natural Selection is no longer operative in a civilized community, it is necessary, if the best are to survive, for some form of artificial selection to take its place. Unfortunately the tendency at the present time is towards the production of the smallest families, in every class of the community, where there is a good inheritance to pass on; while the mass of the population is the offspring of parents who have a poor inheritance to transmit. The " well-born " who are growing up into manhood and womanhood should consider these facts, and realize that they have a duty to the race and a responsibility to all the unborn children.

INDEX

(An asterisk indicates a figure.)